THE MAGIC WITHIN

Avoiding
Self-Deception
In Recovery

Mary Lee Zawadski

Health Communications, Inc.
Deerfield Beach, Florida

Mary Lee Zawadski
Self-Discovery
Randolph County Hospital
Roanoke, Alabama

Library of Congress Cataloging-in-Publication Data

Zawadski, Mary Lee
    The magic within: a book on self discovery/
by Mary Lee Zawadski.
      p.   cm.
    ISBN 1-55874-030-9
    1. Co-dependence (Psychology) — Popular works.
    2. Self. I. Title.
RC569.5.C63Z38 1990   89-28331
158′.2—dc20   CIP

©1990 Mary Lee Zawadski
ISBN 1-55874-030-9

Publisher: Health Communications, Inc.
        3201 S.W. 15th Street
        Deerfield Beach, Florida 33442-8124

Cover design by Keith Pierre

Dedication

To Dad and Grandma Dina — I love you.

To my brother Tom for helping me with this book.

To Mother, Tom and Cathy for your struggle with life and your courage, strength and understanding in your recoveries.

To Denny, Kris and Tommy for your hard work on your recoveries and the unconditional love you have for me and each other.

Contents

Introduction

Who are you angry with? Who are you blaming? Whose feelings do you feel responsible for? What are you telling yourself about being alone? What price do you pay not to be alone? Are you willing to put up with any behavior not to be alone? Did you get married to make yourself happy? Did you buy a dress or car or take a job that you felt would make you happy? Did you move to another town because you blamed the town for your feelings and behaviors? It isn't working, is it?

How are you treating your spouse? After having the children you wanted so badly, how are you treating them? Are you exercising compulsively? Are your relationships

with others squeezed in between going to different types
of therapies? Is there balance in your life sexually? What
types of relationships do you have with other people, the
opposite sex as well as the same sex? Even though you
have numerous years in sobriety, is life still miserable for
you? Does it feel like you are failing at sobriety?

We need to stop working against ourselves and to learn
what to do and *how* to do it. We have to become aware
of what it is we do so that we can change. We cannot
change the reason that we try to avoid pain. These reasons
may become an excuse system for us rather than something to help us change. In my many years in this profession I have seen many people who used all these reasons
as excuses to stay irresponsible. For instance, I used the
alcoholism of my parents and my brother as an excuse for
many of my behaviors, feelings and attitudes. Then I
could always blame them when things went wrong.

It is important to take responsibility for our own behaviors, feelings and attitudes instead of putting the blame
elsewhere. When this is done, then healing in us can
begin. For most of us who lived in families of depen-
dency/addiction we were not taught to be responsible
for ourselves and our behaviors, feelings and attitudes
but instead we were taught to look outside of ourselves
for the answers. We told ourselves we would be different,
we would not live our lives the way our parents did. We
left our family system to find happiness, peace, freedom.
We went looking for this in our relationships, jobs, friends,
children, etc. At times we felt that we were finally going
to find happiness but for many of us this lasted only for
a short period of time and then we would find ourselves
going back to the feelings, behaviors and attitudes that
we had promised ourselves we would change. Even
though we are living in completely different situations,
we still behave as if we are in the original system that
began our dependencies.

We, the millions of adult children who have lived with
dependency/addiction and/or dysfunction, are tremen-
dously hurt, angry, lonely, sad, depressed and fearful

people. What we know best is pain. It is our constant companion. Because we have experienced pain for so long we have learned to deny and delude reality, to try to experience the least amount of emotional pain. We have done this for so long it is now not only how we feel but it has also shaped our attitudes and behaviors. It is our reality. To be free from that pain you have to know how to go to it, find it, become responsible for it and then make the necessary changes. This book will tell you how to do just that. If you are genuinely tired of being hurt, angry, lonely, sad, depressed and fearful, it is time to take the responsibility for your own recovery. Even though you have all the power necessary for recovery, you cannot do it alone.

After we take charge of self, we must learn to accept responsibility for ourselves. As soon as someone says to us, "What are you willing to do about you?" we act surprised or hurt and reply, "Me? I have to do something about the pain I'm in?" Being victimized by our background, we have told ourselves that everyone else has to change. The denial, delusion and defenses we have maintained say, "It is not me who needs to change, it is everyone but me, if only they would change I would be fine." Because of this belief we have attempted to change those around us so that we feel better. Some of us have done this for years and years and we are now very tired and have lost all hope of finding happiness. Some of us believe that life is pain.

We are the only people who can discharge the pain that is causing our problems. We have the *Magic Within*. We have had the capability because we have free will, but we have not had the knowledge to know what to change and how to change it. When we are taught how to live life by someone who is imbalanced because of dependency then an imbalanced life is the most we can achieve without further help. We are not taught to be responsible and accepting or that we have the power to change. Is it sensible to be angry and blame our parents because we do not have any balance in our lives, when all they taught us was what they knew, imbalance? Were we aware that they had no balance? At times we questioned their behavior, attitudes and feelings and when we did this, we were laughed at, punished or made to feel responsible for everyone's pain.

The reality is we have the *Magic* that no one can take away, no matter how imbalanced, crazy or sick we feel. We just do not know how to use it. This is what you can learn from support groups, therapy groups, counselors, therapists, psychiatrists and other avenues of guidance. We need to find the balance in our lives. In order to do this we need to study what our survival techniques are so that we know what is wrong and then we can look for guidance so we can change ourselves. We must know what needs to be changed before we can do anything about it. Then we can be taught how to change. If we knew how to do it alone we would have done it long before this but, even with guidance, we are the ones who must make the changes. *You have the Magic Within you.*

1

The Study Of Self —
Beginning Recovery

When we begin to study ourselves, we need to be detailed and specific. We may have trouble with some of the answers because we do not want to be responsible for our behaviors, feelings or attitudes. The first step to getting well or beginning our healing is taking responsibility for how we feel, think and behave. We need to begin to be responsible for *what is*. What is the reality, not our denial, delusion or defenses. What is, not assumptions, maybes, coulds, shoulds, buts or tries. What we learn from dependency is to avoid what is and to remain the victim of the dependency. We try anything rather than admitting what is, blaming our mom or our dad, sisters, brothers, friends,

co-workers, police, judges, bosses, society and other people, places and things. We have learned to expect external sources to take care of our internal needs. When we
take responsibility, it is for someone or something outside
of ourselves. We believe that if we can get all people,
places and things outside ourselves straightened out, then
we will not have to be hurt, be angry, be afraid, be
lonely or whatever else it is we want changed.

As part of our study of self we will examine our
negative feelings, behaviors and attitudes, taking negative to mean whatever feelings, behaviors and attitudes
work against us to find the balance in our lives. We will
examine the energy we give to others and how we do
this. We will look at how the negative feelings of sadness,
anger, loneliness, rejection, blame, etc., are a burden and
drain us, leaving us feeling tired and worn out. We will
study how to be responsible for our hurt, pain, fear,
anger, etc., and how to clear ourselves of them. We will
discuss how to know which feelings we will not be
responsible for, and how we will relinquish our responsibility for them by discharging through talking, crying,
screaming or whatever your guide recommends.

We need to study what we make excuses for and how
we do that: What gives us the right to push our particular
dependency, our anger, viciousness, dishonesty, fear and
depression onto others. Is this okay?

Lessons

One of the lessons that I learned in my recovery was,
whatever feelings, behaviors and attitudes I was putting
out to others, I was getting in return. My grandmother
used to say, "What goes around, comes around." I was
surprised many times because everything I was putting
out I was getting back. I would put out my negative
feelings, behaviors and attitudes and that is exactly what
I would get back. But when it came back to me, it
seemed different somehow. It was okay for me to yell
and scream at my husband but it was not all right for him

to yell and scream at me. I would tell him that I had a right to yell at him because I came from a family of alcoholics but he should not yell at me because I came from a family of alcoholics. We get back what we put out and when it comes back, we don't like it. We believe that everyone else should put up with our feelings, behaviors and attitudes and we use our living with dependency as the excuse, defense or rationalization of this belief.

When we are asked, "What are you going to do about you?" we blame others and whine that if everyone would just behave the way we want, then we would be okay, as if we were the victims. This is not true. What we need to know is, no matter how anyone else behaves or what they say or do, we can still feel good about ourselves and our lives. We do not have to be in pain because someone else is. Some of us end up doing nothing about ourselves and live believing we are the victims of other people's feelings, behaviors and attitudes. Isn't this what dependency teaches us? If you want to stay in the dependency and not change, that is your choice but you are responsible for your choice.

I worked in a hospital where I would be asked to see a person who was physically sick on a medical floor. Many times these people had made choices not to change their addiction/dependency and were suffering the consequences. For them, a stay in the hospital was their only relief from the pain. We attempt to blame our therapist or group, God or our father, mother, husband, children, etc. However, we alone are responsible for our dependency as it is. It may well have been our father, mother, husband, etc., who initiated the pain but that was in the past and we are still reacting as if it is in the present.

Results

As a result of our study of self we will begin to see the reality about us and the patterns we form, what is, not our excuses, defenses or rationalizations. We cannot heal through someone else, for someone else or for the good of others. Many people have believed this and have changed entirely for someone else only to end up angry because the other person or persons were not grateful enough. When we get to *what is* within ourselves, we will find that we will speak from the I and not from the we, us or they. This is the only way we can heal. To get to the I we must stop searching externally for the answer and know that the *Magic is within* ourselves. And then we will understand we have all the power and energy necessary to heal, be happy, be peaceful and make choices. Part of our dependency is that we want to wait until someone comes along and does the work for us. We are fearful to find out about ourselves, some are embarrassed and many of us feel guilt and shame for how we think and behave. Understanding and forgiveness of ourselves is part of the *Magic Within*.

Keeping A Journal

To begin the study of ourselves we will need help and guidance. This can take many forms. For example, it is helpful to keep a journal of what we do and how we do it. To begin the study of self it will be helpful to make a decision that you will be honest about what you record in your journal. If you find that you become embarrassed about something or do not want to tell the truth, then for the time being do not write anything about this and move on to something you can be totally honest about.

Get a notebook of any size or shape or just write on loose-leaf paper. At the top of the paper write one of your feelings, behaviors or attitudes. For example, write *Anger,* then proceed to write anything about your anger that you are aware of. Write "anger with mother" and then write your feelings such as, she makes me so mad when she tries to tell me what to do, she has no right to tell me what to do, she can't stay sober so why does she think she can tell me what to do, etc. Continue with this writing down everything about this feeling you are aware of.

At first this will take time but as we become aware of all the different parts of ourselves, we will become disciplined to record as much about ourselves as possible. We can do the writing by ourselves but the next step of the study of self requires guidance and we will then have to make ourselves be responsible and ask for help.

Remember, you alone have the magic of knowing the information on how you feel, believe and behave but you may not have the tools to know what to do with the information you have gathered. This is where guidance is needed, to help you see what needs to be changed and, specifically, how to make those changes. Do not let this frighten you.

In my recovery I found that it was harder to stay dependent than it was to change. Fear is part of life. It can be used positively to initiate change or it can paralyze us.

There will be many different guides in your recovery process, from all walks of life and from many of the different helping professions.

Writing in a journal and keeping a record of how we feel, believe and behave help in two areas. First, it gets the information outside ourselves so that we can see and discuss it. Second, we can use it as a guide and reference book to know what worked and what did not. When I started my journal, I wrote in it at night. Then, as I became more excited about it, I wrote in it anytime I felt I needed to record the information I had gained.

Outside Guidance

In the quest for becoming responsible for ourselves, we have to learn to listen to ourselves about what we think, what we feel and how we behave. We have the answers to all the questions: *The Magic*. Once we learn how to get the answers, we have to ask for help for what to do with the information. I did not know how angry I was and how it showed in my behavior and thinking until I began to keep a written record of my anger. Then a pattern began to form about my anger which scared me because I did not know what to do with the information. This is the point at which we need to ask for help and guidance. Then we should record how we specifically make the change in each area: feeling, thinking and behaving.

One example of guidance that I received was instead of being sarcastic, look for something good about people and compliment them about it. This is not as easy as it sounds, especially when I always looked for things in other people whom I did not like. But I did what I was told and gave compliments. The people I complimented were as surprised as I was when I did it because they were so used to me being sarcastic. It felt strange to me to look for the good in someone. I was afraid that people would not like me and I had learned that being sarcastic with people pushed them away. This was exactly the opposite of what I wanted to happen, I wanted people to like and accept me. In making this change, I would record in my journal how it felt for me to give compliments, what I told myself about doing this, what my change in behavior was and how the other people reacted. After a time it became easier and easier for me to give compliments and others began to be more relaxed around me.

Change takes time. This is important to remember so that you do not become frustrated and revert to old behaviors. People in dependency generally have very little patience and, once we make the decision to ask for help and start recovery, we want to be fully recovered and have our lives balanced in a few short weeks.

Listening To Our Inner Self

We all talk to ourselves internally. It is part of being human. We listen to our inner self to make decisions, think things through, make judgments, store information. The inner self is made up of our belief systems, our attitudes, feelings, likes/dislikes, rules, laws, etc. The inner self is divided into different parts. They can consist of anger, fear, pain, guilt, shame, grief, control, happiness, peace, repose, quiet, calm, etc. Our inner self will tell us most of the information we need to begin our recovery.

When you study yourself and begin recording in your journal, you will have to listen to the inner self to know how you feel and think and how these make up your behaviors. Because of our denial and delusion, we will need help from a professional to learn how to listen to ourselves. We will need feedback from others to put together our feelings, thoughts and behaviors. This becomes easier as we progress in counseling and learn to discipline ourselves to be responsible to share our inner self with others so as to get guidance as to what needs to be changed.

At first it feels awkward because for so long we have tried to ignore our inner self and cover it up with defenses, denial and delusion. Some of us feel silly and embarrassed to be writing down and sharing ourselves with others. After all, we are breaking some of the major rules in our family of dependency. Do not let anyone know; ignore your own needs and keep the focus off of yourself. As we begin to penetrate our own defenses, denial and delusions, it becomes easier to study ourselves and share it with others. The information begins to flow out of us and we can share it and ask for help with it. It feels wonderful. We can see the light at the end of the tunnel, we begin to experience periods of hope and peacefulness and we become eager to go on to the next change.

Verbalizing

In order for us to get the entire picture of how we think, feel and behave, we need others to help us by observing our behaviors, listening to our words and both seeing and hearing our feelings. It is our responsibility when we begin the study of self to start talking and sharing about how we think and/or feel.

Sharing with others is the beginning of asking for help. When we choose a trained professional to begin helping us, it is important we take the risk and start talking.

Some people I have treated have come to me for help in both individual and group therapy. When they come into my office or group room, they sit down and will not talk or share about themselves. There is no other way to begin healing. The only way you will know what is wrong and what needs change is to verbalize and talk about you and your feelings. There is an old saying, "You are as sick as the secrets you keep." How your healing begins and how it progresses depends on how willing you are to open up and share about how you think and feel.

Accepting Feedback

We need others to tell us how we behave, feel and think so we can gain knowledge into what needs to be changed. For the process of change we need feedback. We ask, "How do I look when I am angry? Who do I blame, how do I sound?", etc. When we begin to ask for feedback, we need to be careful who we ask. Those we ask should be working toward their own balance in life. A common delusion in recovery is that if we receive help and are sincerely working on recovery and take responsibility for all the changes that need to be made, we will never have to feel negative feelings again. These are feelings, behaviors and attitudes that work against us and drain us of energy. You may have already heard someone saying how they never feel hurt or angry since they began recovery. Life has pain, hurt, anger, sadness, loneliness, fear and rejection in it. It is what we do with these feelings when they occur that makes the difference and puts balance in our life.

Listening

An important part of our recovery process is to learn that we need to listen. Listening may be hard for us as we have learned to tune out or hear only what we want to hear. We feel this protects us but it maintains the delusion. When we tune out, we shut off the listening inside us by thinking of something else, fantasizing or we can tell ourselves that what the person is saying is dumb or stupid. Others listen for a short time then tune out while they go inside themselves and prepare a reply. To these people what they are going to say is more important than what they hear. What needs to be done in order to listen is first to focus on what is being said, look at who is speaking, keep yourself open and then let the information in. Ask them to repeat if it is necessary for you to receive the information clearly.

When I first came into this profession one of my duties was to show Father Joe Martin's movie *Chalk Talk*. I showed this film every Wednesday night for three years. I could repeat his words verbatim. One thing I learned was that if I listened instead of thinking I knew everything, then I could learn something new from the movie every time I saw it. As we listen to ourselves and others we need to study how we sound, how we feel when we hear others and what behavior follows this. After a time we will begin to see patterns forming.

Discipline

Once we have asked for feedback and begin to listen to it then we need to discipline ourselves to find out what it is about us that needs to change. Many of us are great procrastinators. We need to start slowly, not expecting to become disciplined in three days. Remember, recovery, a process to find balance in our lives, takes time.

One of the easiest ways initially to discipline ourselves is to write in our journal. We need to write about our feelings, behaviors and attitudes. Writing in the journal itself becomes one of our disciplines. As we become more disciplined we will recognize and learn to celebrate our achievements. To celebrate simply means to take credit for the work you have done, then relax and enjoy the changes you have made and the decision you made to be responsible. As you gain more and more energy from making changes in your life, you will have time and energy to do the things you always wanted to do with your life. It is so exciting! You can do anything you want to do when you take responsibility for you. You've got the *Magic*.

2

Our Past History

Recovering From Addiction

People who have been in remission from their addiction and still feel depressed, angry, sad, hurt, sorrowful, guilty, ashamed, etc., silently live in terror that this may be all they can expect from life. They believe that being in remission from their addiction is enough. Because of this belief, when their life does not change much, they feel they have failed and are ashamed. They will not or cannot ask for help. They have worked very little on putting their life in balance in all other areas. They will need to begin a study of self to see what needs to be changed and how specifically they can become responsible for the change.

Depression

In my personal experience, I became severely clinically depressed after my initial intensive treatment. I felt
so ashamed to let people know that I wasn't feeling well
because I felt I had failed recovery somehow and some
people behaved as if I had failed. But I'm glad to say that
there were others who understood and guided me in the
direction I needed to go to begin healing the depression.
I was against psychiatry or mental health institutions
because they scared me. I knew that if I went to "one of
them" they would lock me up and throw away the key.
Then everyone I knew and loved would say, "I knew
Mary Lee would be locked up some day."

However, I knew deep inside that I needed to ask for
help and accept guidance. I ended up on a psych ward,
yes, a *locked unit*, and I can remember the loud noise the
door made when it was shut and locked. Through this
experience I was forced to trust in someone and something that I feared. I was in the unit for five days, being
very ill with depression. Those of you who have been
clinically depressed will identify with the heaviness, hope-
lessness, helplessness, terror, darkness, troubled sleep,
panic attacks, eating disturbances, etc., that are part of
clinical depression.

I had not eaten for six days, I had about four days of
constant panic attacks, I was afraid of everyone and of
everything. I knew I had to face whatever was wrong
with me so I asked my brother to take me to a hospital.
I was too tired to fight any longer. Being in that unit was
a turning point in my life. I had to accept many things
that I had tried to avoid accepting. I had to accept that I
was depressed and that the depression I had was a mal-
function in my brain chemistry, accept psychiatry and
the mental health professionals, accept that they knew
what they were doing, accept that I had to be responsible
for being on medication, accept that I was not weak or
crazy, accept that I had not failed in my recovery, this
was just another part of it. I was taught that there were

many aspects to my dependency and each piece would be changed in a different way with different guides. I became aware that one way is not the only way.

It was frightening to be locked up, but at the same time I knew I could not continue as I was. People from outside the unit treated me very strangely when I was there. I had visitors who would stand a long way from my bed and say things to me as if we were strangers. They would talk as if they were afraid I was going to "lose it." I knew they were afraid of me so I told them they did not have to stay. I became aware of how hurtful and lonely it is when people know you have a mental illness. The two people who were not afraid of me were my children. They climbed up on the bed and sat by me and hugged me and told me they missed me and they loved me. How grateful I was to be loved so completely and sincerely. I cried.

I was grateful for the experience. I grew so much from the experiences of being admitted to a lock-up psychiatric unit. I took responsibility for being depressed, I risked and trusted my doctor, I accepted the help I needed and trusted that they knew what was best for me to heal the depression. Many of the fears I had attempted to cover up in my life were faced and I took responsibility to ask for help and make the changes I had been guided to make. It worked, and I felt a lot of freedom and also had the energy to go on to the next stage of my recovery.

Suffering

How do we suffer? What or who makes us suffer? What are we victim to? Are we martyrs? It is important that you begin to study and record in your journal the answers to these questions. Generally our first reaction to these questions is, I do not make myself suffer, others make me suffer. Then we have a long, long list of who it is and what they do to make us suffer. We are taught by our dependency to be a victim and all victims suffer. I was very quick to let everyone know how I was suffering by having my parents and brother as addicts. In treatment I became really angry when I was told, Mary Lee, you are a martyr and like suffering. Only you can change you, you cannot change them. I said to myself, I don't like to suffer, but what can I do, my family will not listen to me? I really didn't like the way I was but it was all that I knew and I really did not know what was wrong with *me* or how to make any changes. The dependency had been passed down for generations and I believed that life had to be hard, sad and angry.

We do not consciously want to be sick or to suffer, but we have been molded into certain behavior, attitudes and feelings that create this belief. Instead of focusing on who we are victim to and why, we need to focus on "what is" within ourselves. Instead of continually taking time to decide who we blame, we need to begin to focus on ourselves. After all, haven't we focused everywhere but ourselves up to now? Is it working?

To begin recovery from our dependency we have to surrender to win. We are not Sleeping Beauty with a prince out there who is going to kiss us and make it all better. Our responsibility in recovery is to ask for help. We cannot do it alone although many of us would like to. If all we needed was ourselves, we would have been well a long time ago. If you are not already involved in therapy or a support group of some kind, take the responsibility and do it. It might be scary but you have lived in fear all of your life, you're good at being scared. It will be necessary in your recovery to have the support and guidance of people like yourself or someone who has been trained in the treatment of dependencies.

Our dependency isolates us. It teaches us through shame and fear not to share the secrets. It teaches us through arrogance and self-centeredness that we do not need anyone's help and not to ask for anyone's help because we can handle our own problems. Asking for help is the most important move you can make toward becoming responsible for your recovery, now and in the future. When we take the big step and admit we have a

problem, we have advanced beyond the other dependents out there who are still in denial and delusion.
There is hope for all of us. In the years I have been in this
profession I have helped guide many people. When they
would begin to feel sorry for themselves or begin looking
at what they had to change as being too hard and start
telling themselves that they could not make the change
needed I always told them, "If I can do it, you can do it!"
They discovered the *Magic Within*.

Learning The Rules Of Our Dysfunctional Families

To survive we acted as if we were happy and smiled,
or were quiet and unnoticeable. We were defiant or
extremely obedient. Our behavior depended on our own
particular circumstances. In a home of dependency, the
problem is that the rules change every 15 minutes, depending on the stage of our parents' dependency.

In my own case, the rules were different when my dad
drank two beers than they were when he drank eight
beers. This could happen in a matter of one to eight
hours. When Mom had one Scotch versus four, the rules
changed entirely. For me to survive that constant change
I had to become very quick at knowing which stage they
were in. I became very good at it. I could tell where they
were drinking, how much they had to drink and with
whom they were drinking. Whatever stage they were in,
I knew which survival technique I needed to use in order
not to be hurt by their drunkenness.

I would prepare myself for when my dad came home.
I hated this because if he had been drinking hard liquor,
he was scary due to the unpredictability of his behavior.
No matter what it was, if the TV was too low or too loud
or a fork was laid on the table incorrectly, he would start
yelling about something. He would bring up the past,
such as an "F" I had received on a report card two years
before or the milk I had spilled the previous week. Or he
would go into a rage over something he had created in

his drunken mind. Sometimes he would get everyone in the house out of a dead sleep, yelling and throwing things as we watched in terror.

Survival Techniques

At that time in my life, it became necessary for me to replace terror with a survival technique. My technique for this was to tell myself, "I'm not afraid of you and you are not going to hurt me." This dialogue with myself meant I felt the least amount of emotional pain. I became so expert that I could determine by the blinking of my dad's eyes, the slur of his words or the expression of his face how affected by alcohol he was. As a result of these signs I knew what I had to do, when I had to do it and how it had to be done in order to protect myself.

Leaving Our Family System

Many of us who lived in dependent families could not wait to get out and be on our own. We wanted to prove to the others in our family what we could do. We wanted to prove that we did not have to live as they did, or treat our children the way we were treated. We set out to show them how they should have lived their lives. We did not and do not live our lives for ourselves, we are living to prove a point to our parents and other family members. Some of us are frightened to use any type of alcohol or drugs because we fear becoming addicts like our parents. Others drink or use drugs to prove to their parents they can control their using. If these people become addicts, they may have a hard time admitting to their addiction because, not only did they fail to prove their point to the addicts in their family, but now they are just like them and they had always said, "I'll never be like Mom or Dad." A heavy sense of failure and anger accompanies their denial.

The Body Has Left But Not The Spirit

When we physically leave our family system, we still remain there in feelings and attitudes. We take all the anger, fear, pain, guilt, loneliness, sadness and rejection with us. They are our burdens. Our delusion is to believe that when we leave this family system, all that will be left behind. So we carry all this extra weight with us into our adult lives. Some of us leave physically, but never really leave mentally or spiritually. Because we do not know how to be responsible for our changing we continue to use the survival techniques that we used in our childhood to experience the least amount of emotional pain.

When something negative in our adult lives happens we use the same old denials and delusions we used when we lived at home with our addicted family. If a relationship partner confronts us because we are crabby all the time, we blame it on our families. If we are unhappy and cannot get a good job, we blame our families, if we are moody and cranky with our own children, we blame it on our families. When we go into a relationship we do not go in willing to work on a relationship, we go into it with all the extra weight we are carrying from our families of origin.

Being in a relationship with us is heavy, we have so many hidden agendas from our families. Our belief at this time is that our adult lives are unmanageable due to our families of origin. The reality is that we are causing our own pain by clinging to outmoded survival techniques.

There's No Escape

We are still dependent upon our original families of pain, and continue to believe that if we can just make them happy, or do the right thing to please them, then we will be free of pain. We focus on them much of the time and keep constant contact with them to see what caretaking we think we should do. I married when I was 20 years old and was glad to have my own home where I did not have to be afraid most of the time. I was glad to get away but I continued to have daily contact with my family because I was fearful that without my caretaking, they would harm themselves or others. The same fears I had in my original family system I continued to have in my second family system. This dependency causes problems in our relationships as we continue to put the family of dependency before anything or anyone else in our lives, including ourselves. Even though we have left physically, we are still dependent on them. We can be in the best mood and be with our partner or friends then the telephone rings and it is one of our family members, telling us that Dad is drunk again and we can hear him in the background yelling and swearing. We become fearful as if we were right back with them, our defenses go up and when we hang up the phone, we are a different person, our whole mood has changed. Then, we push the anger and fear that we are feeling on whoever we are with.

Others see us as moody, and they become confused and hurt by our behavior. When they confront this behavior, we blame it on our family of origin. The cycle continues and can get so bad that people in our lives stay away from us and partners leave us because our behavior is too hard to live with. Sometimes we leave our partners because we think that they just did not understand. If we marry into another family of dependency, there is constant anger, fear and arguments about each other's families. The denial and delusion stay intact. There is no confusion because both people in the relationship feel, behave and believe in the same thing. When we come from a family of dependency and marry into a family of dependency, having no relief from the chaos of dependency confirms for us that life is hard and life is pain.

Suicide — One Way Out

Many adult children of addiction/dependency between the ages of 25 and 35 begin to have suicidal thoughts and either plan or attempt suicide. This can occur because of the realization that our lives are not what we want them to be. We begin to hear ourselves sounding like our parents. We notice our behavior is not what we wanted it to be and are aware that the negative feelings are still with us. In our delusion we have said we will never live like them, we'll show them how they should have lived, our life will be better because we will leave this family. So we leave our family system to go into our adult lives to show our families how they should have lived. We form relationships, we marry, have children and begin to hear ourselves, then we become scared. The more fearful we become, the more defensive we become. Some of us attempt to fight harder to prove that we can live differently from our parents. Sadly, this will catch up with most of us and we will either choose to seek help or continue on and progress in our delusion and die believing the delusion.

I went on like this until I was 29 and tried to kill myself because I was tired of caretaking. I did not know that I didn't have to take care of others. I believed that if they all died or participated in treatment, I would be done with them and no longer have to take care of them. My brother had been in treatment and was sober; my father was dead as a result of his addiction, and my fears, angers, hurts, etc., were not changing. I was very frightened and did not know what to do.

The reality was I was not changing. What I was doing was replacing the original people that I had taken care of with new people. My belief was that life is pain, there is no relief. I felt so heavy, so sad, so hopeless. I would look at my husband and children and see only burden and fear. I would feel guilty because I could not make them happy. I wondered how much more I had to do for and with them before I would feel some relief. I did not know if I could go on. Each day it was harder and harder to get the energy to function. Each request for my time and energy was a new burden. I felt sad and irritated when asked to be a part of anything. I felt sorry for myself and would say to myself, "Why doesn't someone ask me what

I want? Why doesn't someone take care of me and let me rest? Why do I always have to do everything? How can I get some relief from all of these demands?"

I began to sleep to escape. I had no awareness at this time that there was any way to change what I was doing. I did not have the tools to ask for help and receive it.

My decision to leave this life of pain came as a relief at first. Then as I began to think of my children having no mother, my husband having no wife, my brother and sister having no sister, I became angry with myself and got the courage from somewhere and made the internal decision that I was going to fight for my life and be happy, whatever that meant. Ironically, at that exact moment the telephone rang and it was my brother Tom. He started out the conversation by telling me he was very concerned about me and that he had a number for me to call so that I could get some help. He said, "I have been worried about you for some time. You appear to be empty and hopeless. I want you to know that, *I love you* and I will do anything I can to *help you*." I began to cry and sob. Tom had been sober for five years or so and I had felt like I had lost his love and here he was telling me he *loved me* and would *help me*. I did not tell him I was planning suicide. As I cried, deep sobs came from within me. I felt so grateful and, for the first time in a long time, cared about and loved. Tom gave me a number to call; it was the number of a therapist. My first reaction was, I don't really need to see anyone, I am okay now. But I did what I was told, called the number, made the appointment and kept the appointment. This was the beginning of my recovery.

Surviving, Not Living

We have learned to survive life, rather than live life. We have done well learning how to survive. We have learned different techniques so we experience the least amount of emotional pain and fear. When we realize that the very survival techniques that used to work for us no longer produce what we want out of life, we make continuous attempts to change, but do not feel better. Unable to shed these techniques, we become consumed with the terror of being out of control. Instinctively, we continue to use these survival techniques, compulsively without choice. We find ourselves doing things, feeling things and thinking things that we do not want. For some of us this is our bottom and, like myself, we ask for help and begin our recovery process and finding the balance in our lives.

An Example Of Leftover Survival Techniques

Denny and I have two children. When they were born, I was happy and made many promises to myself about how I would raise them. I would show my mother and father how they should have treated my sister, brother and myself. I would always listen to them, I would play with them, I would attend all their school functions, I would never blame them, holler and scream at them, call them names that hurt their feelings and on and on. When they were still babies, about two and four years old, I began to hear myself and how I was hollering at them and calling them brats, and making them go to their room for no reason except that I was angry due to something that was taking place in my original family system. I began to see and hear how I was sounding and behaving with my children. It was the exact opposite of what I wanted to do. I began to fear this behavior and worked harder and hard to stay in control. I could do all right for a while and then if a lot was happening with my original family system or with my husband, Denny, I would feel and hear myself taking it out on the children. I would pray to God every night for help to stop treating my children this way, then terror would set in. I would beseech, "Please, God, help me to be nice to my children." The guilt and pain were tremendous.

One morning I woke up and there at the end of my bed stood my two beautiful children, who were five and seven years old. They were both smiling and lovingly they wished me a happy birthday, climbed on the bed and gave me a big kiss. My daughter told me to get out of bed because they had a surprise for me in the kitchen. They each took one of my hands and led me to the kitchen, singing *Happy Birthday* to me. There on the kitchen table was a pretty placemat, wild flowers they had picked for me in a vase, cereal in a bowl, milk in a little pitcher and toast on a plate with butter and jam. Also on the plate was a piece of paper which they had colored and decorated and it read, "We love you Mommy." I can remember their big eyes, one pair of blue and one pair of brown, filled with unconditional love.

All I could do was cry as the guilt and terror engulfed me. I was screaming to myself inside, you do not deserve their love. How can you treat these beautiful children, who love you so much, so harshly? I made a vow that I would never yell at them, send them to their room or call them names again and I meant it with all my heart. By two o'clock that afternoon I had already broken my vow. Then I could understand how my parents must have felt. I remembered many times when my father would be full of remorse because of his drinking and promise us he would never drink again and that he would take us places and buy us things. How he would cry when we bought him presents. As a child I did not understand this, I would feel so sorry for him and want to make him happy so he would not cry. I did not know or understand that he was causing his own pain and at that time he did not know how to change it.

As reality starts to intrude, these techniques we use to lessen pain become less effective than they used to be. We feel the need to strengthen and harden them into full-blown defense systems. The cycle continues, and we have to work harder to prove that we are in control.

I hope that in reading this chapter you have begun to understand the problems you carry from your past and why you need to change. This is not a quick fix book. It takes time to heal. The pain we feel is uncomfortable. We are always in a hurry to fix ourselves and others. The title *The Magic Within* means what it says. We need to take care of ourselves through our own *Magic* and with the help of others.

3

Our Defense Mechanisms

Lack Of Self-Worth

Self-worth is very simple. It means being responsible to ourselves. For some of you right now this
sounds very confusing. Self-worth has little to do
with whom we marry, where we live, how much
money we have, how hard we work. We can think it
does, but that is a delusion. When dependents say they
have low self-worth, in essence what they are saying is
they have no self-worth. We gain self-worth when we
choose to be responsible for what is with us. This
happens when we are accountable for what we say,
what we do, what we feel, what we think.

One of the first ways to develop self-worth is to ask
for help. When we do this we admit that we don't know

what is best for us. Some of us will seek help in a matter
of days, while others will suffer for years before seeking
help. If we are honest we admit we have known for a
long time that we were not okay. Many addicts have
known for years that they have had a problem with a
chemical but denied this and set out to prove they
could handle their using. Dependents do the same
thing. We know we have problems for a long time
before we do anything about it. We must prove to
ourselves there is nothing wrong. So when you ask for
help you have already gained self-worth. Reading this
book is an effort to get help.

Self-Worth Is Not What We Do

Many people hide behind their profession as they
search for self-worth. For example, some physicians,
attorneys, judges, counselors, nurses, policemen, parole
and probation officers and other helping professionals
believe they are immune from dependency because of
their occupation. Instead of being themselves, they live
through their profession and have no balance in their
lives. Their self-worth is based on helping others.

Many Adult Children of Alcoholics (ACoAs) who become parents do the same thing and their self-worth
depends on how their children behave, look and feel.
These people become rigid and controlling with their
children because it becomes very important that their
children are perfect so they, as parents, look perfect.
These parents suffocate their children with what they call
"love." They are at the school as much or more than their
children, they pick their children's friends, they do not let
the children have choices, much like it was for them in
their families. Because they don't drink or verbally or
physically abuse their children, these people believe they
are healthy parents. My son quit school when he was 17.
I put myself through so much pain in terror of what
people would think of me as a parent. For three days I
cried, yelled, cut myself off from others and became

depressed. Not once did I think of my son and how he might feel about his reasons for quitting school. My family would see me cry and ask what was the matter and I would say, "Nothing." I gave my son dirty looks and said to him, "How could you do this to me?"

We can become so fearful that we become self-centered. It doesn't matter to us about anything or anyone else, just ourselves, how others think of us and what we might have to do or not do. We are unable or unwilling to see how others are affected. After three days I finally called my counselor and began putting myself and my son down. I was angry, hurt and full of terror. When I told him I didn't know what to do with my son, he asked, "Have you asked your son what he was feeling or if he needed to talk with someone?" I said no and began to feel an enormous amount of guilt and began declaring that I should have known what to do in this situation. My counselor simply said, "How could you have known, you have never had a son quit school before." So I asked for help, received guidance and took responsibility for my feelings, attitudes and behaviors.

There are some people in a recovery process that believe they will be able to handle everything in life that comes their way. What I found to be very important to me in my process is realizing that I do not have to know how to be responsible for everything life may have in store for me. What I am responsible for, is admitting I do not know, asking for guidance as to what to do about the situation and following the direction I am given. To be able to recognize that we do not know what to do is recovery, asking for help and taking direction is finding the balance in your life. When we are willing to do this, most of us will find that in being responsible we no longer have to be in continuous pain and fear.

Disaster Planning

In living with dependency, negative feelings predominate. Disaster planning is a learned belief, that all of life and experience for us and the people we love will end up or come out in pain. We don't have enough money, we will never have enough money, everybody hates us and always will, we are no good and never will be, nobody loves us, we aren't worth loving, we will never be loved, life is unfair so what is the use, why try. What do your disaster plans consist of? We are unhappy and we tell ourselves and others it doesn't matter. I want you to realize that, yes, it does matter. You want to be happy and it matters.

We look for it outside of ourselves and year after year happiness doesn't happen for us so we learn to disaster plan in an effort not to feel the pain and disappointment. Somewhere and at sometime in our lives positive things have happened but when they take place we negate them by saying this isn't going to last, so don't get used to it or expect any outcome from it. Any positive feelings that we have we qualify and we turn them into a negative belief. If we plan something or are looking forward to something, we disaster plan so long that by the time it occurs we have a negative attitude and can say, "I told you this wasn't going to work." This disaster planning is an effort to protect ourselves from negative happenings. We disaster plan because experience has taught us that positive feelings never last or that positive feelings are followed by many negative ones that cause us pain.

So we believe that we should not enjoy ourselves too much because it will not last. We are not easy to be around, we are always griping, bitching, whining, pouting and anticipating disaster so that by the time the event happens, we get what we expect and can only focus on the negative. For dependents disaster planning is a technique we use to ease fears and lessen our anxiety. This gives us the illusion of control. Begin recording in your journal how you disaster plan and what fears and anxieties you tell yourself you are alleviating.

Denial And Delusion

We learn our alibi system from our families of dependency. For instance, both my dad and mother were alcoholics. Each of them had a different alibi system. Dad drank because his dad was abusive, my mother drank because my father was abusive. My brother drank because both his parents were abusive. I got depressed, fearful and angry because both my parents were abusive. My sister had many fears and whined all the time because her parents were abusive. This is how the victim in us blames others and goes on blaming until they become responsible for the changes that need to be made in their own lives. The victim generally wants everyone to change for them.

The alibi system begins to collapse as time goes on and people no longer believe us. We become more elaborate with our alibis and they turn into defenses. A defense is whatever we use to cover up what is really happening, actions we use to shield ourselves so that we will not be found out. Defenses help us to build walls around us so that we can experience the least amount of emotional pain. We box ourselves in and at first this feels safe and comfortable because we believe nobody can hurt us. As the years go by and we continue to box ourselves in, our safe and comfortable little box can become a trap. We may not be able to get out of our box until we choose to be responsible for changing what it takes to get out of our trap.

It's Them, Not Us

We have the belief that someone else has to change so that we will not feel trapped. We begin to think "if only" and develop what I call our wish list. Some examples of our wish list are: if only they would stop drinking or taking drugs, if only I could find someone to love me, if only I could get the right job, if only I could move away from all this, if only I had money, if only I could be a parent, if only he or she would change, etc., etc. We begin to attempt to control ourselves and others to make our wish list come true. We work hard at this and, for a short time, we believe we are finally happy. When a short time passes and we realize that we are still feeling the pain, we do what we know best and we start to blame everyone and everything again, become miserable and are back in our trap. This continues over and over again until we become so defensive we are hard to live with. We get angrier, more depressed, more hurt and our fear turns to terror and we feel crazy. Most of us have a fear of being crazy because we have made many attempts to feel better and never do, so we label ourselves crazy. Others of us have been called crazy. When this occurs we begin living day after day, attempting not to look and feel crazy. This can become a vicious cycle. The harder we work not to look and feel crazy, the crazier we look and feel.

We have the *Magic Within* to change all of this but we do not know it. We feel as if life will always be this way. To stop the vicious cycle, we need to ask for help. However this is done, and it varies, we do need others to help us to find the balance in our lives. We may need to admit that we do not know what is best for us and take on the responsibility to follow the guidance of those that do.

Most of us have been focusing outside of ourselves for so long looking for someone, someplace or something to remove our pain from us. We carry the burden of others with us. When we feel responsible for their outcome, sobriety or happiness or are waiting for others to make us happy, then we feel continually tired and burdened. So tired, in fact, that everything we must do in day-to-day living becomes a great task. We become angry because of this burden we feel we must carry. Each one of us has learned a behavior to escape from this. It gets worse as the years pass. We pray for rest, that everyone will just leave us alone but that is not what we really want. We do not know what we want and we begin to feel helpless and hopeless. We may begin to cry much of the time and we may think of ways we could escape our present situation. We have exhausted ourselves in an effort to find happiness for others so that we will be happy.

Denial

Denial means that we refuse to believe the truth, refuse to recognize the truth and take responsibility for it. To remain in denial we must begin to be dishonest. We are dishonest first with ourselves and then we lie to others. We are liars by the very nature of dependency. Denial continues as we progress in our dependencies and it becomes more and more elaborate. We are now lying to cover up lies and we become anxious about what we said to whom. We begin to be confused within ourselves about reality. Denial becomes so elaborate that we move into delusion. Delusion means that we believe what is not real. We have lied for so long to so many, including ourselves, that the lies become our reality. This becomes recognizable only when we move in recovery to be responsible for our "truth" which penetrates denial and delusion. Then and only then can reality be faced and changes made.

Effects Of Denial

Denial and delusion are used by us to suffer as little emotional pain as possible. They have to be penetrated for us to heal. Remember the box that we are trapped in? Some walls of our trap contain denial and delusion. In denial the feelings and behaviors do not match. We say we are not angry, but we are sarcastic to everyone, we say we are fine but we cry all the time. Our bodies begin to react to the stress that is created by the denial and physical problems can occur. Some common ailments include anxiety, depression, headaches, sleep disturbances (sleeping all the time or unable to sleep), back pain, spastic colon, ulcers, etc. The list is endless. Many dependents go from doctor to doctor hoping to find out what is wrong with them. When all the tests that are taken to see what is wrong with the body come back negative, depression and fear are common. So the person goes to another kind of doctor and the cycle can be endless.

We are being dishonest and in denial, the head does not match with the gut. A war occurs internally. It is never our fault and we use up a lot of energy proving this by lying, blaming, yelling, crying, etc. We can spend our whole lives finding out who is at fault instead of living our lives. If we could only see and hear how we look and sound when we deny. We really believe what we are saying and it is so sad to watch this happening to people. It can get so bad that we verbally and physically abuse others to protect our own denial.

Inside us we are confused and scared. We don't know what to do with reality so we must deny that it is happening. Our body must be telling us something is wrong because we get sick. Our body gets sick to caution us that we are deceiving ourselves. When we are confronted on our anger, we yell, "I am not angry," with our jaws clenched and all our muscles tight. We don't want people to see that we are angry so we deny it. When we are confronted for this we experience fear that we are being found out and we don't want fear because it is emotional pain. We blame whoever confronted us for making us angry and believe that we now have the right to punish them.

In the treatment of my dependency the first thing the counselor worked on with me was my anger. I was in denial of my anger and I really believed that because I was not calling people dirty names, being sarcastic or pushing people around that I was not angry. I had told myself in my teens that I was not going to be a bad person which I understood to mean angry. When the group started confronting me on my anger I was truly confused and felt they were picking on me. I began to defend myself the only way I knew how (with anger) being sarcastic, swearing, blaming, etc. and each time I did this they asked me if I was angry and I would say, "No, but if you keep picking on me I will get angry and it will be your fault." They didn't accept this and continued to confront me. I was baffled. "What do these people want from me?" I would ask myself. I attempted many times to tell them what I thought they wanted to hear and it still did not stop them confronting me.

One day in group one of the other patients that I had become close to started by calling me names and yelling at me. The counselor kept asking me, "Are you angry yet, Mary Lee?" After attempting everything I knew to stop him from this I bolted up out of my chair and ran toward him calling him every name I could think of. When I was halfway across the room the counselor said, "Are you angry yet, Mary Lee?" It took this much for me to begin to penetrate my denial. I began to cry and felt so hurt but the group loved me despite my denial and this was one of the first feelings of acceptance I had experienced.

As we become aware of the obstacles along the road to recovery — alibi systems, defense systems, lack of and the search for self-worth, disaster plans and denial and delusion — we will learn to take responsibility for the *what* and *how* of our words and actions. We will begin to find balance in our lives, the *Magic Within* us.

4

Our Feelings
And Our Reactions

Pain

When we are hurt we suffer mental or emotional anguish. In a family of dependency hurt is created by broken promises, being ridiculed, having no privacy, being used, being lied to, being forgotten or ignored, seeing drunken behavior, having to lie to others, having to sneak, etc. The accumulation of hurt creates pain. The inability to heal the hurt maintains the pain. Pain is what hurt can become inside us.

Causes Of Pain

In most families of dependency promises are made and not kept. Did this happen in your family? How did that make you feel? The reality is that much of the time

43

we were hurt. We may feel vulnerable to others if we talk about our hurt, sadness or pain, because we may cry. We learn to not share these feelings due to this. It can become a "they win" feeling. They hurt me again — they win. It gets stored and eventually we can start acting out destructive behavior, as if we need to do something to get even or survive. It can be so powerful and present such a strong power base that many children from dependent families when they become parents treat their children the same way as they were treated by their parents. It can come out in any of a number of forms; child abuse, spouse abuse, drug or alcohol abuse, eating disorders, etc.

When we experience hurt we assume that those around know we are hurting. This is difficult for others to confirm unless the person who feels the hurt states that they are hurt. Too many times we deny or repress the hurt and we will chastise those who want to help us when we are in pain. A child approaches their mother or father to help because the child sees crying and remorse and assumes they can help the hurt. Their help is rejected with statements like, "Leave me alone," "If you were never born I would not be in this situation" or simply, "Go away." Now we have a person that has learned not to help those who hurt because it will hurt back if you try. When this child becomes an adult they may be seen as non-supportive by their family, friends or self. What they learned from the family in pain is that to be supportive only creates hurt and pain in them.

Now there is a new generation who feels the pain and hurt of others but does not know what to do with it and they have hurt and pain themselves because of it. They may ask themselves, "Why can't I help like others do?" "Why can't I be a good partner?" They may become caretakers, going out of their way to prove they can help those who hurt others, placing their own needs second to those who hurt, placing their own needs second to those in hurt or pain. If their help is refused they can become angry with the person needing help and look for someone/anyone who needs their help. These people become dependent on helping others with their hurt and/or pain.

Why do you feel the need to help others? Do the helpless anger you and do you turn away from them? How do you feel about needing help from others? What do you do with your hurt or pain? You can ease your pain by recognizing it, by using the *Magic Within* you.

Remember that better than anything else, we have learned how to experience emotional pain. When we live with dependency, pain is always present, there is little or no relief from pain, we get overdosed on pain as children.

Pain Is Sadness

Many describe the feeling of pain as a sadness. It is sad to feel that nobody loves us. We feel sad when our affection is not returned, when the only touch we get from our parents is a slap or a shove. We feel sad when we rush home from school one day, bursting with pride at some new bit of knowledge we have gained and wanting so badly to share this with our parents. We want so badly for them to feel proud of us and love us. So we share our excitement and our parents immediately yell, "Quit bothering me, I am busy, you are always causing trouble, what is the matter with you, are you stupid?" Or they are not there mentally or spiritually for us; one of them may be passed out on the couch, they are treating each other with silent anger or they are fighting again.

We may feel sad when we hear the sound of our parent opening the can of beer, the bottle of scotch or a bottle of pills. We know it will change them and we are fearful. We know that it will affect their ability to hear, talk and understand us, it will affect their ability to be our mom or our dad.

My mother and father usually went grocery shopping on Saturday mornings. I would get up early just so I could see them before they started to drink. It was a happy time for me to see my parents not drinking. Mother would make out a grocery list, they would speak to each other in a nice way, sometimes laugh, sometimes ask me about my life, sometimes tell me I was a nice girl. Then mother would say, "We are going grocery shopping and we will be right back." It was sad for me to hear this because I knew they would not be right back. Broken promises but as much as I heard them over and over again I would want to believe that this time what they said would be true. They did not come right back most of the time. Sometimes it would be midnight or 1 a.m. There would be no groceries, no mom, no dad. I would call several of the bars I knew they went to, only to be told by the bartender they were not there, or they had just left. Sometimes one of my parents would come to the phone and angrily tell me to stop calling, they would be home shortly. It is painful to be lied to over and over.

It is painful to be sad. Sadness in the families of dependency is the result of knowing something is wrong but not knowing what that something is. We grew up watching sad faces, hearing sad voices and feeling *heavy* sadness all around us. Perhaps you felt that nobody loved you. We may feel sad when our affection is not returned or understood. Mother was so sad at times that she did not have the energy to listen. We would kiss our parents goodnight and they did not return our affection, they kept looking at TV or would smell of alcohol. When feeling remorseful about something he had done while he was drunk my dad would cry, and I would feel sad for him. When mother would cry because of the bills that could not be paid or because my dad was not home yet, I remember being sad.

The continuous sadness builds into pain for most of us from dependent family systems. This sadness permeates our lives and gradually builds into pain. We carry it into our adult lives, into our relationships with others, into our future. We may overcompensate by always acting happy, even when we are not, and this becomes a delusion or we can enter into what I call the "sad zone" and stay there causing our lives and those around us to be uncomfortable. Somewhere along the line, perhaps after physical abuse or being called hurtful names by someone we love, we made a decision to defend ourselves from that pain. As children of dependency we told ourselves, "I cannot handle the pain." We finally decided to protect ourselves and not feel the pain any longer. To accomplish this, we had to do whatever it took for us to experience the least amount of emotional pain. Some of us defended ourselves, some isolated themselves, some became depressed. Pain can manifest itself in many different ways. The way we protect ourselves from emotional pain can also manifest itself in different ways. Learning to feel again and be responsible for our feelings, behaviors and attitudes takes work, hard work, but the outcome can be wonderful. We take the pain with us in all our attempts to have intimate relationships, who we become, what we feel and in our interactions with others. Our belief system becomes *life is painful*. Pain manifests itself in different people in different ways.

What Is Pain?

To begin the study of pain it might be helpful for you to list some of the people, places and things that you know have caused you pain. There are both past and present feelings of pain. Keep the list as specific as you can. The more specific it is, the more manageable it will be for you to identify, record, share and make changes. Some examples are:

> I felt pain when my mother would start mixing a drink.
> I felt pain when my father would lie to my mother.
> I felt pain when my parents would argue and call each other terrible names.
> I felt pain when my father would cry when he was confronted about something he did while he was drunk.
> I felt pain when my little sister would start to cry when my parents would argue.
> I felt pain when mother would cry because the bills could not be paid.
> I felt pain when anyone would call my father a drunk.

I felt pain when my father had to go to jail.

I felt pain when my grandmother would tell me everything will be okay.

I felt pain when I watched my brother start drinking.

I felt pain when my father and brother would fight and
break furniture and I heard the sound of flesh hitting
flesh.

I felt pain when I would watch people I love be drunk
and unable to function. They would stumble, trip,
have slurred speech and be unable to eat without
slobbering all over themselves.

I felt pain when I watched my husband take a drink.

I felt pain when I looked into my children's eyes after I
had yelled at them.

I feel pain when someone is nice to me or others.

I feel pain when people are unfair to others.

I feel pain when I see a person drunk or high.

I feel pain for their families.

As you begin to record your pain a pattern will develop and you will begin to see that some of the pain has
been with you since your childhood. You are probably
using the same defenses that you used then. What we
know best is how to experience the least amount of
emotional pain no matter what the cost. The second part
of the study of your pain is to go back over the list and,
next to the individual cause of your pain, record how
you reacted to it and what you told yourself so you
experienced the least amount of emotional pain. Most of
my reactions and thoughts about my pain were angry. I
told myself in my early teens that nobody was going to
hurt me again. In order to live up to this rule I had made
I became angry, sarcastic, tough, uncaring. What I told
myself is that nothing bothered me, people get what
they deserve, all people are liars and want to hurt me,
nobody really cares about me and I don't care about
them. I carried these attitudes and beliefs around for
years. I really believed that I was doing well — "I'm
tough" hardened into an attitude and after a while the
consequences of this began to enter my life.

Consequences Of Defenses Against Pain

The very things that we believed helped us to not feel pain begin to turn on us and not only do you have the original pain but you now have all the consequences of the defenses that once took the pain away. It is a lot like the way the addict feels as their disease progresses. At one time their drug of choice removed their pain but as they progressed in their disease the drug of choice becomes the cause of pain. Just as the addict in early recovery must look at the consequences of their using so must the dependent, who is not an addict, look at the consequences of their behaviors, feelings and attitudes. Listing consequences makes us begin to see patterns of behavior and what needs to be changed. The consequences for me of being tough were many. People became frightened of me, people were hurt by my sarcasm and didn't want to be around me. This caused me to feel lonely and rejected. Of course I always placed the blame back on them. The nice people gossiped about me and laughed at me, I wasn't invited to parties, proms or school functions by any of the nice boys or to slumber parties, birthday parties, shopping and lunch by any of the nice girls.

I felt so hurt and in my denial could not understand why these people were doing this *to me*. I would try to change and be "nice" for a couple of days but my defenses were strong and hard and all it would take was a dirty look or someone laughing at me and I would go back to my old behaviors. I would tell myself that I was right, that nobody cared and I didn't either. So it went on, day after day. I became harder and harder to the outside world. And I believed inside that life was pain and only the tough survived.

We go into adult relationships with beliefs formed as children. We make attempts at being different but they don't last because we have no guidance on how to maintain the change. Many of us begin to feel crazy because we do not understand why we cannot stop doing what is harmful to ourselves and others. People begin to ask us, "What is the matter with you?" We ask ourselves the same thing and most of the time the answer we come up with is that we are no good and do not deserve a happy life. This hardens into an attitude which leads to us envying and resenting anyone who is happy and enjoying life. I remember many times thinking to myself, "How do people do it?" What I came up with in my head was that all the happy people in the world were really miserable and were faking being happy. I would resent people who had nice things and good jobs and traveled. I would envy them and go back to my "old friend" anger, then go home and be angry with my husband because he wasn't providing me with nice things. I would be sarcastic to my parents and brother and sister because I believed that they were the reason I was not happy and did not have nice things. Consequently, this created a chip on my shoulder and so throughout my adult life, the same things happened that happened when I was a child. People that had nice things and were happy did not ask me to any parties, functions, luncheons, etc. So I continued to harden a little more.

Getting Away From It All

One of our delusions as children that grew up in dependent homes is that as soon as we can get out of here we will be different. Many of us go through our adult lives trying to prove to our original families just how they should have lived and treated others. The sad realization here is that this rarely seems to be accomplished because our original families are seldom grateful enough and usually do not admit they were wrong. They cannot understand the importance of what we are trying to prove. So we end in the same place we started, angry, blaming, sad, hurt, lonely, etc., and decide that it is all their fault.

When we become adults we have more freedom to do what we choose but unfortunately, those of us from dependent families don't know how to make responsible

choices and set out to get other people, places and things
to change so we do not feel pain. We do not have to live
in constant emotional pain. This is a choice and there are
guides that will help you to change this. Even if all the
people, places and things stay the same, you still do not
have to live in constant emotional pain. The key is to
make changes within you, not for you to make changes
in everyone else.

When you study the reasons that you give for your
pain you will begin to see a pattern. You will notice that
some of the reasons for your pain have been dropped by
you, but some of them are still present and new reasons
occur daily. Keep track of these reasons and next to the
ones that are constant, record the consequences. One
way that was helpful to me to study my pain, was to
study how I handled physical pain. When I had back
surgery, I was keeping a journal and I recorded my
thoughts, feelings and behaviors that occurred during
this time. I became aware that I would go deep inside
and talk to myself about the pain. While I did this I did
not want anyone to touch me or talk to me because it
took a lot of concentration to decide what to do about
the pain. I do the same thing with emotional pain. I want
others to leave me alone because I am concentrating on
the pain and what to do about it.

Before I was in my recovery from my dependencies I
only had negative information to base my decisions on.
Therefore, I was unable to change the pain. In the physical pain I had information from others as to what to do
to lessen the physical pain, for instance, lie on your side,
ask a nurse to turn you, rest, relax, do as the doctor
ordered. I did as I was told and, sure enough, I began to
feel better. Soon I could sit up and walk on my own and
the pain went away. The same is true with emotional
pain. In recovery from dependency I had information
from others as to what to do to lessen the pain. I did as
I was told and the pain went away. Now each time that
pain comes into my life I have information on what to do

about it. If that fails to work, I ask for help from those who can guide me to lessen the pain *and it works.*

Removing Pain

Picture yourself in a box which will be your emotional pain. How does the box look, does it have a color, does it have a sound, does it have feelings? Put yourself in the box. How do you look, what are you thinking, what are you saying? Our emotional pain is constantly with us. It begins with a small piece of pain and builds into a mountain of pain because of the inability to know how to change it. It is like having a scratch on your arm. Without cleaning it or dressing it the scratch will become bigger and redder and more painful. This continues until the whole arm becomes affected, complications set in and the rest of the body is affected. Your emotional pain can and will go away. You can feel happy and relaxed, you can live life for you and enjoy others too. Take responsibility for your pain and record it, share it, and ask for help as to what changes need to be made. Use the *Magic Within* you to make your emotional pain go away.

Fear And Fear Tactics

The predominant feeling in a family of addiction is fear. This feeling is the one we work hardest to cover. Exposing it leaves us vulnerable to those around us. We live in fear of many things, of not knowing, living in unpredictability, having no boundaries, people we love hurting themselves or others, losing control of our emotions and going crazy, being wrong, being right, feeling good, bad or indifferent and the list goes on. There is very little sense of safety in the dysfunctional family. The accumulation of fears causes a state of uneasiness, apprehension and distress. This intense fear or dread lacks any cause or a specific threat. When the feeling of fear or concern is detached from a specific source it feeds itself, causing a vicious cycle. This cycle of fear causes us to worry and produces strong mental agitation, such as fear of death of self and others, sirens, police, accidents, other people.

Because of fear, as children we spent a lot of time hiding in closets, under beds or in the basement. We spent extra time at school, participating in athletic activities or clubs, joining gangs, groups or finding heros real or imaginary. We spent a lot of time planning our escape from our family system but felt guilty and fearful that someone would find out these horrendous thoughts. Some of us ran away several times. Some of us never went back. Every person is a little bit different but we are all basically afraid that others will find out we do not know and do not like who we are or our families of origin. We are fearful of getting hurt, of being affected by dependency or our dysfunctional family. Fear is the precursor to anger most of the time.

Types Of Fear

Most everything we do has a fear tactic in it. Basically we fear losing something we have and not getting what we want or need. For instance, I was fearful that my spouse would leave me, that my children would not be perfect and that my mom and dad would die or kill each other when they were drunk and fighting (the latter is a common fear among dependents). I was also afraid that someone I loved would become an addict to alcohol or other drugs and hurt me over and over again. If they became addicts I was afraid I would have to take care of them. I defended my fear well. If I was afraid, I would defend myself by being angry, hurt, withdrawn or by running away. This was due to a rule I gave myself about fear. The rule was: no one is going to make me afraid. Being afraid leaves us vulnerable to the world and our culture does not support those who are afraid. "Be a man, don't be afraid, what are you afraid of? If you believe in your higher power you have nothing to fear, don't you believe?" or "Look at your mom and dad, they are not afraid of anything."

Some of us married young, joined the military or went away to school, all of us *afraid*. We stayed awake in bed, fearful that dad would hurt mom because we were not at home to stop the fighting. When we heard about murders on the news we were afraid that it would happen to someone we loved or ourselves or that we would be left all alone. When our parents left the house we were afraid they would not come back and we would be left alone to grow up or be separated from our brothers and sisters. We can grow up with this separation anxiety, affecting us in our adult lives.

One person told how he had heard about Richard Speck and the murder of the student nurses. His mother was a nurse so he feared for her life. He had trouble sleeping and started wetting the bed again. After everyone else was asleep he would get out of bed to check the locks on the doors and windows. When his mother went out at night, he acted up so that the babysitters would not want to return. Who could he tell about his fear, without hearing the answer there is nothing to be afraid of. He would go inside and say to himself, "But I am afraid. Does that mean there is something wrong with me? I better not admit this to anyone. They could lock me up, take me away, become angry, reject me or laugh and make fun of me being afraid." How many times, in how many children, of how many dependent families does this happen only to affect them later in life. We are afraid of people. We are afraid they will see how inadequate, bad or worthless we are. Yet we are afraid of being left alone even though we usually felt we were.

When I was ten years old, my dad and uncle, both drunk, got into a fight. My dad smashed my uncle's head against the radiator. I remember seeing the blood everywhere. I heard my mother screaming and someone calling the police. When the police knocked on the front door, my dad grabbed me and we hid under the bed. While we were under there he kept telling me to be quiet, "Don't let them know we're here!" He was afraid at the time and later would deny this, leaving me confused. What I learned from that experience was not to tell others you are afraid. I knew my dad had been afraid and I knew he had lied when he said he was not afraid, but believing my dad was a liar was against one of God's commandments, "Honor thy Father and thy Mother . . .," so now I had another fear to add to my group of fears. These fears add up and become so intense that all our energy is used to protect ourselves.

Cycle Of Fear

Part of dependency is to believe that external sources will take care of internal needs. We are constantly looking for the answers to make us feel different outside of ourselves. When we do this for a period of time and become aware that it is not working, we become more fearful and work harder to control the external world. This causes more fear which reinforces our survival techniques. Life becomes a vicious cycle of fear and control of self and the attempt to control others. When they do not do as we say, we begin to punish them and we become fearful of our behavior. Any attempt to change this cycle only works for a short period of time, creating more fear, keeping the cycle going.

Fear Is Not All Bad

Just an additional note about fear. It is not bad and can be one of the best defenses for survival that we have if we respond to it and are responsible with it. Fear keeps us from jumping in front of buses or attacking a person with a loaded gun pointed at us. Rational fear protects our children and keeps us balanced. However, irrational fear is what hurts us. Irrational fear is very real to the person who has it. Change can occur when we take responsibility to ask for help, accept guidance and make the changes. This comes from within and we have the *Magic Within* to help us change.

Fear Can Be Irrational

When we grew up in families of addiction and dependency our parents or guardians taught us what to be afraid of. We believed everything these people told us or showed us. We had no other point of reference. At an early age we already had built-in fear tactics that had been taught to us. As we grew and matured we began to add to these, basing our new tactics on what we already feared and adding new experiences of fear. Rarely did someone teach us that it was okay to be afraid or that we could change ourselves or our surroundings to eliminate the fears. We can learn to accept that parts of life are fearful. When we realize this we need to ask for help and support to accept it. Some fear is healthy and keeps us from getting harmed or harming others. What we were taught about fear is neither healthy nor balanced.

For instance, as a little girl, I would watch my mother's fear when the mail came. At times she would cry holding the opened mail in her hand. Then she would get angry and yell at my dad. I never asked her about this because the rule in most homes of dependency is "Do not ask questions" but I added one more thing to my list of fears . . . the mail. I did not know or understand why but I learned from my mother by observation. As an adult I was still fearful of the mail and the mailman. As I began to get help and keep a journal about myelf and my fears I became aware that my mother was frightened of the mail because the *bills* came. My father did not always have a job so she was afraid of the consequences of not having enough money to pay the bills. As my father's irresponsible behavior with money continued along with his addiction, mother's fear grew. As teenagers my brother and I would have to go across town and get my father's check from his employer. I still remember the looks we would get from the lady that gave us the check. Her look said to me, "You poor things." I hated doing this and added another fear tactic to my list . . . I cannot trust anyone where money is involved, not to have money is fearful.

I continued believing these fear tactics about money and had to be counseled on how to be responsible with money and how to spend money in a healthy way. You too may have to get help to develop responsibility with money. A lot of us either come from families that have no money and are irresponsible with it or families that have a lot of money and use it as a way to manipulate others. For example, each of us in my family had our own fear tactic about money. My brother was afraid of not having enough money and he became frightened of spending any in case it ran out. My sister was fearful of not being able to pay the bills so she would pay all the bills and not have enough left over for food or day-to-day living. I did this same thing and became so fearful of money running out that I told my husband to take care of the money. Then I constantly checked on him to be sure he did it right. All three of us had fear tactics about money and each one reacted a bit differently. This is the kind of information you will get by studying yourself and recording in your journal your behaviors, feelings and attitudes.

What Do You Fear?

There is a fear group inside each one of us and it is important that you begin to record your fears as they come up. As you gather information about what you fear and how you feel and behave with it, a pattern will begin to form. In this pattern you will begin to see that with certain fears you will delude yourself by saying, "Nothing scares me," while with others you go to the other extreme and become immersed in these fears and become helpless and whiny. Neither of these extremes is comfortable to be in nor are they balanced behaviors, feelings and attitudes concerning fear. You will need help and guidance to change what is not working for you.

To begin to change what you fear and how you feel and behave with your fear, it will be helpful for you to

take the responsibility to record and share what you do
with fear. To help you begin I have listed some of the
common fear tactics among dependents:

No one loves me.

No one understands me.

I am crazy and I cannot let anyone know or they will
lock me up.

I cannot tell anyone the truth or they will not like me or
believe me.

I cannot let people know that I lie but I have to lie to be
accepted.

I must tell people what they want to hear.

I hate myself. What am I going to do?

I am afraid to be alone.

I do not know how to talk to people.

I do not know how to be happy. What is the answer?

I am afraid people will find out what I am really like.

I must protect myself but from who? from what?

No one can find out about my family and what they are
really like.

I cannot go on living in all this confusion.

I will not make it in life if I have to be alone or if I have
to be with others.

What am I going to do?

My husband/wife/partner doesn't love me.

I will lose my job.

I cannot face another day.

I must do something to change others around me.

I must stop my loved ones from drinking/using drugs.

I must love my father/mother/spouse enough so they
stop using alcohol or drugs.

I must prove to my partner/children/whoever how much
I love them so they will not hurt me.

I must be perfect so I will be loved by all and never have
to be confronted by others.

I must stop my parents from embarrassing me.

No one can know that I have failed.

I must look good.

I have to have many friends.

I have to be invited to all the parties or functions so I will
be popular.

Now that you have begun your list of fears, the next step is to go back over them and put in the fear tactic that you use, the *or else*. Some examples of the *or else* are:

> I must stop my parents from embarrassing me *or else* I will have no friends.

> I must stop my parents from embarrassing me *or else* people will find out they drink all the time and I have lied about them and I will have no friends.

> I must look good *or else* no one will like me and I will be alone all my life.

> I must look good *or else* people will know how fearful I am and they will not love me and I will be alone all my life.

> I must tell people what they want to hear *or else* they will not like me and I will be lonely.

> I must tell people what they want to hear *or else* they will know that I came from a family of alcoholics.

> I must do something to change the people around me *or else* I will lose control and somebody has to be in control.

> I must love my mother enough so she will stop drinking *or else* people will believe she is bad and that would hurt me too much.

> I must love my mother enough so she will stop drinking *or else* she will die and I will be alone and afraid.

These examples may help you to understand what you need to record in your journal about your fears and fear tactics. Fear is a vicious cycle and can only begin to change when we become more honest about it. Share it with someone who can help guide you to see what needs change. Remember, fear is most often the basis of dependency and you may not believe that it can change, but it can and it dôes.

Take the responsibility to examine your fears and fear tactics and you will find the *Magic Within* you to change.

Anger

In families of dependency anger is always present but
it manifests itself in different ways. There can be loud
acting-out anger, the silent anger, pouting, withdrawing,
dirty looks or the controlled anger, sarcasm, whining,
righteousness and arrogance.

Loud Anger

Loud anger we can see, hear and feel physically, emotionally and verbally. It comes out by yelling, screaming,
hitting, swearing, throwing things, name-calling and accusations. This is generally done to intimidate or manipulate others. Loud anger defends us from reality and
prevents us from being confronted about our behavior.
People with loud anger believe that it is everyone else
who makes them mad so they have a right to do whatever they can to punish or make the other person, place
or thing change to their expectations. They believe that
they have a right to punish others in whatever way they
choose. Living in a family of dependency, anger is always present and we learn how not to be responsible for
our anger by watching and listening. These anger feelings, attitudes and behaviors are handed down generation after generation.

In your journal begin to record your anger, what makes
you angry, how it sounds when it comes out of you and
what you tell yourself inside about your anger and about
the people you are angry with. As you begin recording
your anger, also keep a record of the many consequences
it has. For example, loud anger pushes people away from
us and, for a time, that is exactly what we want. What this
anger does for us in our dependency is to keep people
away. It worked for a while and we were grateful for
that. However, at some point in our lives this anger becomes hardened into an attitude and when we want to
stop it, we are unable to. We find ourselves living in fear
and loneliness. What once worked for us to survive has

now turned against us. We are faced with the reality that we must make changes or everything about us will stay the same. It is very important to write down the consequences that result from your anger. Anger is a human emotion and will occur in your lives many times. What you do with it when it comes up will make the difference.

Silent Violence

Silent violence is anger that is not let out. There is tremendous tension with this survival technique. Nobody talks about it, nobody acts on it, nothing is done about it. We become fearful of saying or doing the wrong thing, of causing an explosion of all this tension. Those of us who have this anger have a righteous attitude that says, "I am not angry. I am certainly not as bad as those that act out their anger." People that I have treated over the years that use this type of survival technique are appalled at the loud, acting-out anger. But, when they become honest with themselves, they find they have planned over and over again how they would act on their anger. In their delusion they still believed they have the right to punish those people that have hurt them. There is no difference about the belief that people are "making us" angry. This type of anger is as powerful as the loud anger except there are no clear rules. With the loud anger there are some specific rules, like, "Get out of the way!" Silent anger is very powerful and it keeps people guessing. Silent anger has no rules so we don't know how to behave with it. Some of us have learned by living in our family to hold our anger in. Either we got punished for it or we were frightened or we received some type of attention for not causing trouble.

Controlled Anger

Controlled anger is a combination of violent anger and silent anger. We believe that we are in control of this emotion. Our ways of behaving with this are more subtle than with loud anger, usually using sarcasm or gossip. In dependent families it is sometimes frightening when we know we are not going to be at a family gathering. What usually happens at a family gathering? The people that are not there are *discussed*. No one in a dependent family system confronts anyone else. They gossip about them and justify it by calling it concern or discussion. We can also become judgmental and label people with righteous judgment. We put people into categories with this type of controlled anger and react to them as we have judged them righteously.

An example of this righteous judgment in my family was: my father drank beer. He worked construction and did not have much money so consequently did not own his own home. Being judgmental, he taught us that anyone with money could not be trusted, "They are only out to use you," anyone having a white-collar job was no good and could not be trusted, anyone who drank other than beer and a bump was a weak person and should be laughed at and also anyone who did not drink was arrogant and thought they were better than others. As a result of this righteous judgment becoming a family belief we were very constricted as to who we could trust, have as friends and what professions we could work in, while asking for help and trusting helping professionals was totally out of the question. So the righteous judgment in our family system led us to believe that if you were not a construction worker who drank a beer and a bump and worked hard then you could not be trusted. Interestingly enough my brother became a construction worker who drank beer and a bump and did not own his own home, my sister married a construction worker and I married a blue-collared, hard worker.

Each of us was caught in the belief of my father's righteous judgment, his anger and the denial and delusion of his addiction. It was hard for each one of us to seek help, go into professions that were not blue-collar and to have friends that did not fit the belief. I used to think to myself that people who did not fit into my father's lifestyle were people I had a right to be angry with and

I would treat them as such. I was very defensive with these people but not sure why.

In a healthy, balanced person judgment is used to make decisions, each option is reviewed and we make a decision within ourselves. For example, we go to a movie and watch and listen. In doing this we decide that we either like or dislike what we saw and heard, then say I did not like the movie or I liked the movie. With righteous judgment, we go to the same movie, watch and listen, the whole time telling ourselves that the movie is stupid, it should never have been put on the screen, etc. When asked if we liked the movie we say it was awful and should be destroyed, the director was a jerk, the stars in the movie cannot act, etc.

Whining is another form of controlled anger, it is "anger coming through a small opening," and is somehow acceptable in the system. I never thought I was a whiner until I saw myself in the movie of my reconstruction *Another Chance* with Sharon Wegscheider-Cruse. I whined a lot, especially if I felt that my loud anger would be punished. Most of it was about my relationships. I did a lot of whining at my husband. All that anger was with my family but I was getting it out by whining at my husband. I married Denny because he was quiet. I remember thinking how wonderful it would be to live in a family where nobody yelled and hit and called each other names. We were married about a month and the quietness I longed for was too much for me so I began yelling, blaming and screaming at Denny, "What is the matter with you? Don't you know how to talk?"

My wish for a quiet family was just that, a wish. I had no tools to live in a quiet family so I began to create what I know best, even though I did not want it. This happens over and over again and creates in us a sense of being crazy. We ask ourselves what is the matter with us. Then we make promises to ourselves that we will stop doing whatever it is we don't like but we can't, so we feel crazy. After a few years of this we begin to prove we are not crazy by doing what we know best; blaming, lying, etc. We must prove that it is someone, something or someplace else's fault so we do not have to be responsible for ourselves. We tell ourselves we are not crazy, angry, sad, depressed, etc. *You make me that way*. With the belief that others are responsible for our feelings our next goal is to convince them that they are at fault. What this does to us is to create anxiety, fear, depression, anger, loneliness, hurt, guilt, etc. The outcome is the same, a sense of being crazy. The next time you are angry begin a study of your anger. What are you saying to yourself and others, how are you behaving and what do you believe about your anger?

Rage

In angry people pressure is formed by holding the anger in. There are many different ways we learn to relieve this pressure, for example, yelling, withdrawing, being sarcastic, whining, etc. For some people, the pressure becomes so great that they self-mutilate for relief. These people admit that they cut themselves, scratch themselves, burn themselves, smash head or fists through walls or windows, have unnecessary surgery, etc. to ease the pressure. Many of us became tough and learned to use our anger to protect ourselves from others only to find that this tactic eventually turns on us.

Continual build up of anger results in rage. Rage is uncontrollable anger. We are afraid of rage for two reasons: Either we will hurt ourselves and others by losing control and going crazy or we will be hurt by someone else's rage. Are you fearful of losing control? How would you look, sound and feel if you lost control? What would others do with, for and about you if you lost control? Would you kill someone, hurt yourself or others? Would you go crazy and get locked up? Begin to study how you feel about your rage.

Living in a family of dependency we are unable to differentiate between normal anger and our kind of anger. The most obvious difference is anger versus rage.

As the child grows up and expresses anger they observe rage that is called anger by those out of control with it. Or this child is so afraid that in order to be heard they have to express themselves twice as hard to get the attention they need. If they are quiet no one pays attention but loud crying, shouting and throwing of things get a lot of attention. They learn that this behavior is responded to over and over again. Attention is attention whether it is negative or positive. All of us need attention.

Sadly enough, the dependent brings this type of behavior into adolescence and adulthood. This behavior is usually supported by the other dependent families that seem to associate with each other. When this adult demonstrates this behavior in other settings, the behavior produces fear, rejection and confusion. For some it means being labeled as crazy or tough. This person is then placed in a lonely situation that creates fear that then makes them even more hungry for attention. Or they find people who understand this anger and stay in this mode. Many will marry or connect with people who are quiet and willing to put up with this behavior reinforcing that this behavior is all right. On top of all of this, reinforcement of this type of behavior can work for the rageful person and they get their way.

Eventually, this rage will catch up with them until they have lost many things. The problem is that the person has done it for so long they do not see anything wrong with it. Rage becomes a part of their person, attitude and behavior. Many times I have had to explain to a patient that what they were demonstrating was not healthy anger but rage. Just as many times the patient will look surprised because they do not realize they are any different than any one else. Working on this can be rewarding because once it is identified as what it is and how it got there, changes can occur. The insight gained by the patient is rewarding for all. Have you studied how you present your anger?

Confrontation

To confront is to describe to a person how you see their behavior and how you feel about that behavior. For most of us we become frightened at the very thought of confronting another person and the rule in the family is: Do not confront and you will not be confronted. This is generally a silent rule. Sometimes confrontation will happen but it is usually when someone is drunk or in a rage or in fear. Doing interventions in my own family as well as professionally made me very aware of how frightening telling the truth can be. We are so frightened of getting punished in so many ways, they won't love me, they will leave me, they will get everyone to hate me, they will just deny the truth. When we start therapy and we begin discussing our family systems, many people become frightened of telling the truth about other family members. They deny problems ever happened and say over and over, "But I really do love them" or "They really are good people."

Loneliness

There are two ways to describe this section. There is feeling alone or being alone. There is feeling lonely and being lonely. One is choice while the other is a state of mind. Many members of a dependent family will feel lonely in a crowd or in their home with people in it. For defense, they choose to or need to separate themselves from those around them. This separation process starts as withdrawing from others. People get used to the withdrawer not participating in life and do not include them. For the withdrawer this reinforces them in the belief that no one cares and they are alone. Loneliness can be powerful because it can be used to punish and/or reject those we feel do not care enough. It also reinforces my feeling that I am no good, therefore all my interpretations of self and others is correct. It is not intentional but is a condition of not knowing what to do about our present lifestyle and not being able to ask for help. The married person whose marriage breaks down in the area of communication isolates himself in the basement recreation room and sits there appearing perfectly satisfied to others. He rarely shares his feelings of loneliness. He gets his human contact at work. At work he looks dedicated to his career. He becomes dependent on his job and may become a workaholic.

Growing up in a dependent family and being lonely, we either became loners or obsessed with doing things, school activities, being involved in a gang, cult activities, or we became victims to persons who thrive on people looking for acceptance and love. We found ways to leave our dependent family as quickly as possible such as going into the military, getting married and sometimes getting pregnant to accomplish this goal. And of course there is the danger of the final attempt to leave, suicide. Being alone is a choice, lonely is a state of mind. We can change if we use the *Magic Within* us.

Rejection

Many dependent people believe that being told "no" is rejection. This is not realistic. We can set ourselves up for constant rejection because we think that people are rejecting us if they don't do exactly what we want them to do. Suppose we call someone and ask them to do something with us and they say, "No, I can't because I am busy." We hang up the phone, feel hurt and rejected and give ourselves messages such as nobody likes me, I will never ask anyone to do anything ever again, the next time they ask me to do something I will hurt them back, what is wrong with me, etc.

This ultimately leads to fear and hate. The fear can lead us to isolate ourselves, withdraw and feel self-pity. The hate can cause us to seek others out to hurt them by gossiping, ignoring them, sarcasm, name-calling, accusations, etc. What has happened? Where does this start?

The Cycle Begins

We need to go back to dependency to answer this. The dependent relies on responses outside of themselves to make them feel good, instead of depending on themselves and their self-worth. In the dependent family it starts with statements of blame by one to another. Examples of this include "Because of you I don't feel good," "If you would only be nice I wouldn't have to drink," "When you are here I feel safe in this crazy place." Many times this will be the message from the parents to the children, teaching them that our feelings come from others. Therefore, we believe that others have the magic and we must get it from them. Simply stated, the belief is because of certain people, places or things I will feel better. This creates the need to find others to hook up with to feel better.

The dependent feels rejected when others don't respond with the magic they are looking for. It is the same kind of rejection they felt at home being second to alcohol and drugs, the alcoholic and drug dependent, the problems of the family, etc. Having this feeling of rejection the person will feel desperate to connect with someone who can fill all their needs that were not met in the family of dependency. We expect one person to fulfill all these needs, in effect putting all our eggs in one basket. We have a relationship and we believe that this one person can make up for all the rejection we had in our original family. We go into relationships with a hidden agenda of how we must be treated so we will not feel rejected. Some examples of this hidden agenda are: they will always listen to me, they will never be angry with me, they will always ask my opinion, they will include me in all their decision-making, they will always agree with whatever I do or think, they will always be sensitive to my feelings and moods, they will always tell me what I want to hear, they will always include me in whatever they do, we will always agree on what friends to have, we will always do everything together, they will never keep secrets from me and the hidden agenda goes on and on. We never tell our relationship partner about this agenda, because we believe that they should just know what we need and expect from them. When they cannot fulfill our agenda we feel rejected and believe that we can punish them in whatever way we choose.

What are your feelings and attitudes when you feel that your relationship partner rejects you? How do you behave? Begin by writing them down in your journal. Another interesting part of dependency is that we have a lot of rules about how others have to treat us but when it comes to us treating others we can do anything we want — after all we were rejected in our family of dependency. Begin to record what your behavior, feelings and attitudes are about the way you can treat others. Can you live up to your own hidden agenda? We need to evaluate our needs and how realistic they are. We need to trust when we are told we are not being rejected, we need to verify with the person we want to connect with what is going on and that it is not rejection. Most important, we need to go inside self and reestablish our expectations of others, our self-worth and our own independence. Only from within can we change.

Guilt And Shame

Shame is different from guilt. With guilt there's a reason or explanation, such as, "I am bad because my dad drank." With shame we are bad. There's no reason, we're just bad people. Guilt and shame are passed down from one blaming and martyred generation to another. For example, we beg one parent to do something about the problem, saying, "Why don't you leave him or her?" We are told, "Because of you kids I have to stay. You need a mother and father." From that time on, any pain, hurt, sadness or fear felt is our fault. In an attempt to change this we strive to get good grades, clean the house, cook for them, get jobs to help with money problems or be extra good. But no matter how hard we try it is never good enough: the pain, the hurt, sadness and fear still remain.

A recovering alcoholic with a shaming spouse tries in vain to make up for those years of their illness. The spouse never forgives them for their past actions. The alcoholic brings home the check, calls to report their whereabouts so the spouse doesn't worry, buys gifts because they are "grateful" for the spouse allowing them to stay in their life. They are driven to overcome this feeling of shame but do not know it. The spouse feels powerful with this and in many cases unintentionally encourages it to continue. If it has been handed down from generation to generation neither person needs to have done anything like abuse alcohol but the behavior of shaming will still be there.

In many cases this behavior can be a result of generations being dependent on traditional values that no longer fit. The women who were told all mothers should stay home with their children but find themselves out working or wanting a career, the man who makes less money than his wife and was raised that men should be the bread-winners, the professional couple who do not want children in order to pursue their careers and were raised that giving their moms and dads grandchildren is the next thing to godliness and so on, all experience shame. The problem is these people can be affected by this and not know what is causing their feelings of shame. It will be important to determine our values with our guides' help.

In trying to deal with shame we either attempt to become so good no one will blame us or else we don't care if we are bad and become defiant and get in trouble all the time. It is a problem that perpetuates itself unless we discover the *Magic Within* us to help us remove the burden of shame.

5

Where Are We Now?

Depression

Depression is a dark place where we feel trapped with no way out. It is heavy, and it is difficult to go on. We feel as if no one cares. We wonder if we're going crazy or even if we're not already crazy. Nothing matters anymore. It is too much to bear. Some of us cry all the time, some sleep a lot or some wake up in cold sweats. This behavior is numbing and paralyzing. Everything we do feels like an enormous effort. Just getting out of bed in the morning sometimes seems more than humanly possible. We are modeled to depression. We watch one or both parents become depressed from using chemicals or because the other is using. Some of us were even given positive strokes for being quiet and depressed. Every day we have to fight just to function. We feel we cannot tell anyone because

73

no one will understand. Because we fear that others will find out, we work even harder to keep up the facade.

A Case History

When we become depressed we revert to old defenses that we learned and used when we were in the dysfunctional family. This often surprises and confuses those around us because it is so different from our behavior when we are okay. My brother had 18 years of sobriety and was married 20 years when he went through a divorce. He developed a new relationship, experienced a lot of changes on the job and became disconnected from his support system and immediate family. The result was his becoming clinically depressed. He did not know what was the matter but he did know he felt bad. He reverted back to his old behaviors, anger, sarcasm, withdrawal, paranoid thoughts and ideations. As a result he asked for help to make some changes. He trusted his guides and gave up his new relationship as it was, began psychiatric therapy and was placed on an anti-depressant medication.

In therapy he started to understand what had transpired and how many stressors he had taken on while denying their effect. After all he was a former counselor, a member of Alcoholics Anonymous, and the Executive Director of the Behavior Health Services of a major metropolitan hospital. How could he be depressed? And how could he afford to be depressed when so many people, places and things were dependent on him? When he asked for help his recovery began and he became aware of what had happened. He was able to see how this denial and delusion had kept him trapped in depression. He did not have active thoughts of suicide but complained of being afraid he could not do his job or have a relationship. He felt desperately alone and obsessed with needing people. His appetite was fine, and he slept well — too well. He was afraid these symptoms were not those of someone who was depressed. From what he had learned he had thought he was just going through a stressful time. His AA group was no longer enough because he could quote and say the right things in an AA meeting after all these years. Fear was prevalent and he became preoccupied with it, mostly the fear of being alone.

Coming out of the depression was just as hard as going into it. He discovered that even though he was in recovery from his chemical dependency, he still needed to work on the problems he had from being raised in a family of dependency. This surprised most people including myself. After all, hadn't he helped me and hundreds of others in his work as a counselor? He was recognized nationally in 1984 for his work in the field of chemical dependency and employee assistance programs by *Esquire Magazine*. But this was part of the problem. He looked good and did not believe this could happen to him. He was so convincing to others that no one suspected his fear and depression.

Depression is not to be taken lightly and just turning it over is not a total answer. It took a psychiatrist, medication, AA and a men's support group to help Tom. He was also surrounded by people who understood mental health issues and were supportive of his diagnosis, treatment and recovery. He discovered that the magic wasn't in his relationship, in the job or in his dependency on others or they on him. He discovered the *Magic Within* himself. (In his recovery he visited me at my home and assisted in the writing of this book. He shared with me that the contents of this book helped him enormously to gain insight on where he had been and where he could go if only he understood and worked at it.)

What Is Depression?

There are many definitions of depression. There is a chemical depression when the brain chemistry is imbalanced. There is suppression of feelings that causes depression and there is modeled depression when we grow up in a family of dependency. We watch and hear depressed people so we model the depression and assume it is normal behavior. Symptoms of depression include poor concentration, inability to concentrate, agitation, irritability, sleep disturbances, anxiety, an increase or decrease in appetite, low energy level, low sex drive, suicidal thoughts, despair, thought process disturbance, inability to think clearly. This list names a few of the symptoms and they should not be considered a catch-all or as a way to diagnose yourself. If you feel emotionally depressed you need to check it out and let a trained professional determine the cause. Many people from families of addiction describe their depression as being a dark, cold, small place. Begin to record how depression feels for you so you can recognize it.

Grief

As a dependent person grief occupies a large part of our life. There are many different kinds of grief. There is grief experienced every time there is a sense of loss. Grief is experienced not only because of the death of someone dear to us but also because of other senses of loss. It can include a lifestyle change, divorce, giving up an addiction, giving up a dependency, a loss of job, a change of job, loss of excuses, defenses, denial, delusion, attitudes, behaviors and feelings. Even having to move to another house, job and/or school, which many of us from dependent families had to do as a result of living with someone with addiction, can cause grief. With each type of grief there are different stages.

As you begin the study of your individual grief you will begin to see patterns forming. This will be helpful to you because you will see what needs to be worked on. A chosen guide will help you to work on these areas of your grief. To better understand grief and how you behave, feel and think with it we will review some of the stages of grief and give some examples. As you identify the various stages of grief record them in your journal. As with anything in life there are many different theories on grief. I will give you the theory that was most helpful to me in my recovery.

Stage One

The first thing that happens is that we are in a place of disbelief. We say to ourselves, "Is this really happening?" We feel overwhelmed, confused and frightened. This phase or stage can last anywhere from hours to a few days. An example of this for those of us in families of addiction is that a painful experience happens as the result of someone we love using alcohol or drugs.

In my family when he drank, my father would hit my mother and call her names. On one occasion they became very loud and the neighbors came to the door to ask if everything was all right. My father then began an argument with them. He told them it was none of their business and pushed the neighbor away. The neighbor began to fight back and then more neighbors came to see what was happening. Everybody was yelling and screaming and hitting each other. The police were called and they came to the house and took my father away in a police car. My mother began to cry, yelling at the police that they were taking the wrong man to jail. She then began to yell at the other neighbors who were standing around. She called them names and told them to mind their own business. The neighbors were looking at me with such pity in their eyes and I became angry and took my mother into the house. Then she called some other family members and they came over. They began to drink and started planning to go to the police station to get my father. Then they began to argue about how they would accomplish this. They began to get louder and louder and started pushing each other and once again a neighbor called the police and the police came to break it up. While they were at the house this time, my mother and uncles started yelling at the police and calling them names. The police told everyone if they did not go home, they also would be arrested.

My mother and I went back into the house and the telephone rang. It was my father. He was yelling at her to come down and get him out of jail. My mother told me to stay home with my brother and sister and she would be right back with my father. I was in a state of disbelief. I felt overwhelmed, confused, frightened and angry. While my mother was at the police station getting my father, I sat in a state of disbelief, unable to make any sense out of the happening. I felt numb.

When my parents returned, they began to discuss the happenings. They too were in a state of disbelief, over-whelmed, confused, frightened and angry. They had both been drinking and they began to discuss how it all took place. Once again, they poured themselves a drink to discuss the events and once again, they started to argue. I knew that all of this took place as a result of their drinking, but as I sat there and listened to their denial and delusion, I began to believe what they were saying. I told myself that when they got up in the morn-ing, they surely would never drink and argue again (my denial and delusion).

The next morning I went to the kitchen and found both my parents in a state of grief and remorse. Nothing was said and we all just sat there in a numb state. Still in my delusion I believed that they would never drink and argue like that again. As the morning progressed with their denial still intact, they each poured themselves another drink. I went back into a state of grief. I grieved for the loss of parents who were sober and in control of themselves.

As people living in dependency we are in a constant state of grief resulting from the continual loss we expe-rience. Some of us remain in this stage of disbelief until we seek help.

Stage Two

Each day, we grieve the loss of reality over and over again. A five-year-old child sees his father drunk and out of control which affects the father's ability to walk and talk. The child asks his mother what is wrong with his father. Fearing the truth will hurt the boy she decides to lie and tells him his father is tired. Two months go by and the same little boy is over at a friend's house and sees his friend's father behaving in the same way that his father had and he asks his friend, "Is your father tired?" The friend replies, "No, he is not tired, he is drunk." The little boy goes home and tells his mother, "Timmy told me that when daddy acts funny he is drunk, not tired." His mother yells at him and tells him never to say that about his father.

As this little boy gets older, he sees a repeated pattern of people calling his father's behavior drunk and doesn't say anything to his mother. When he hears his mother telling others how tired his father is, the little boy feels grief and sadness for his mother. Then, as he gets older, the grieving for his mother's delusion may advance to the anger stage of grief. The boy gets angry every time he sees a drunk or whenever anyone makes excuses for a drunk. The little boy, now a man, is still in a state of grief.

Begin to record in your journal all the memories you have of this stage of grief for you. Remember to be as honest as you can in keeping your journal. Honesty will help you to begin healing faster. Start with how sad you feel when you see or hear someone you love in delusion or denial and you want to say to them, "Please see the reality" and they cannot. To begin the study of your delusion and denial you will need a guide to help you.

Stage Three

Another stage of grief is when the emotions about our loss surface. This can happen in a matter of hours, days or weeks and sometimes in the families of dependency, years. Without any warning these feelings well up in us and an uncontrollable urge to express our grief comes out. Can you remember any time when you felt suddenly sad, angry or had some other feeling and you did not know where it came from? Because we are taught by dependency to not allow our feelings to happen but to defend, deny or delude them, these surges of grief come out with no warning. Healthy people are taught how to allow these feelings to come out as they happen and therefore they are not filled with urges to grieve uncontrollably.

I loved my grandmother very much. She was always there for me. She cooked, sang songs and attempted to give me some relief from the fear that occurs from living in a family of addiction and dependency. I was so very grateful to her for this and I was kind to her and protected her in return for her love. Even when I became an adult I still deluded myself that my grandmother would be with me forever and I would love her forever. She died when she was 90 years old and I was an adult. I did not grieve her death for many years. What I did do was deny that I felt anything about her death and acted as if I was strong and in control. Inside I was very angry that God took my grandmother instead of one of the alcoholics in my family. My reasoning was simply this: She was so loving and kind and all they caused was pain, fear, anger and trouble. I focused my anger on God and the alcoholics in my life. Many times throughout the years of my denying my grief for my grandmother I would lash out at the alcoholics in my family. I would want them to hurt as much as I did because my grandmother was gone.

I remember the night she died. We all went over to my aunt's house and they began drinking and I screamed at them that I hated them and wished they were dead. I yelled at them to stop drinking because my grandmother would not want them drinking on the night of her death or at her funeral and I was going to see to it that they didn't drink. I ran from the room crying and so full of anger. At the time I believed that they were making me angry. I went out on the patio and prayed to God in anger, "How could you take my grandmother from me and leave me with all these people that drink?" Years and years passed before I really allowed myself to grieve for my grandmother's death. In all those years I remained angry and bitter. Occasionally these feelings would well up in me and come out uncontrollably at the people in my family that drank. How heavy that is to carry with us.

Almost exactly the same pattern of grieving surfaced when my father died. He was only 51 years old and he had been sick for about a year. His stomach was very large, his body was all swollen and his skin was turning yellow. I remember feeling very fearful but my denial and the denial of my family said he was just eating too much. I would watch him struggle to get out of a chair and have trouble with his breathing when he walked. Nobody talked about his condition. We would tease him about his big belly and he would laugh with us. I saw the fear in his eyes and I wanted so badly to go to him and hold him and tell him how much I loved him. I wanted him to tell me he loved me and everything would be okay. This never happened. He died of cirrhosis of the liver; in effect he died of alcoholism. My pattern of grief repeated itself. I was angry that God did not take somebody else instead of my dad. I loved him so. Even though he drank and his alcoholism affected many of us, I wanted him to live and some other alcoholic in my family to die. Again, I did not show my feelings at the funeral or for years after. The welled-up feelings came out uncontrollably at other people, places and things.

After my father died I became angry with anyone who drank. I told myself that no one was going to hurt me again. I thought I was keeping my feelings under control. They began to come out at my husband and children and many times at my mother who was still drinking. Have you had anyone you love die? What did you do with the feelings? How did you keep them under control? Begin studying how you felt inside, what you told yourself, how you behaved and what you believed. Write all this down in your journal.

Stage Four

The next stage is to feel alone and depressed. Most of us in families of dependency experience this stage of grief much of the time and it can go almost unnoticed. This stage of grief defines who we are, alone and depressed. Because it is so much a part of us, we only recognize that we feel more alone and more depressed as more grief comes into our lives.

Stage Five

The next stage of grief is that we may experience some physical problems due to our inability to grieve. Most people who cannot continue through the different stages of grief complain of physical problems. However, not all people have physical problems due to the inability to grieve. Some of the most common complaints are headaches, back pain, menstrual cramps, digestive tract problems, i.e. ulcers and colon problems. Many of these people go to doctor after doctor and have test after test. None of the tests show any problems. This causes anxiety in the person because they begin to believe they are crazy or that they are making themselves sick. At this time many physicians will refer their patient to a psychiatrist or a therapist to work on their emotions. The sad thing about this for people of dependency is that only a small percentage will follow this guidance. Instead they change doctors and continue to deny that anything is wrong with them emotionally. Society has put a stigma on emotional or mental problems. The stigma is that you are considered weak, defective or inferior and it will stay with you forever. In families of dependency an effort to seek help is often sabotaged by ridiculing, embarrassing, criticizing, shaming and minimizing of the problem by other family members. Seeking help under these conditions can be lonely.

Stage Six

Feeling anxious and fearful is the next stage of grief. We have done everything that we know to stop the grief and we are still experiencing it. We begin to feel as if we are crazy. We feel tired much of the time. No matter what we try to do to change how we feel, we continue to feel bad. We make great efforts to look, sound and feel normal. Inside we are fearful that people will find out that we really are crazy. We are also afraid we will have a breakdown. For some of us, this can continue for years. At times like these, sometimes all we want to do is run away from life. We want to hide so no one sees how crazy we really are.

People tell us to get involved in something new and exciting and that is the last thing we want to do. We make attempts and, when we fail, it just seems to make us feel worse. Some of us put all our energy into just making it through the day. The opposite can also be true in this stage. Some of us get overinvolved in everything and are so full of anxiety that we cannot rest or relax. We have to be around people all the time and the thought of being alone and quiet is very frightening. When we are alone, we have the TV or radio on constantly or we are talking on the telephone. These are all attempts not to be alone. We are scared of having time to think or feel. Begin to record in your journal the anxieties and fear in this stage of grief.

Stage Seven

Feeling guilty is the next stage of our grieving. We think of what we could have done, should have done or would have done a million times over in our head. We replay the losses in different ways in an attempt to find out what went wrong. We also attempt to find what it is that we did or could have done to prevent the loss because we feel at fault and, at times, are even told that it is indeed our fault. We feel guilty and work to make up for our guilt.

When children are blamed for the father's drinking, which led to the loss of his job, which led to no money, which led to their mother crying, these children work the rest of their lives to make up to their parents for all the losses they feel responsible for. This is very sad. People work the rest of their lives to make up for something they are not responsible for and unable to live their lives for themselves. They have the belief that as soon as they get it right, then some relief will come. For some, this does not happen and life to them is a struggle with constant emotional pain.

Anger And Grief

Anger is a healthy part of grief. When the person does not work through this stage, they can become resentful and hostile. Unfortunately, many of us from dependent families stay in this stage for a long time. Many consequences occur as a result of unresolved resentments and hostility. Also, we are modeled by our parents to be resentful and hostile. We watch, listen and feel the hostility and resentment in our parents. We see them act out their hostility and no one seems to say anything. No one talks about this behavior and the child's belief system becomes one that says I can push my anger anywhere and on anyone I want and that is okay. The children grow up, get married and begin to verbally and physically abuse their families believing this is okay. If they should suffer any consequences from this behavior they feel as if they are being picked on. I have had many people tell me that the police in their city have nothing better to do than wait for them to make a mistake. These people believe that the police are picking on them. They truly believe what they are saying.

A Light At The End Of The Tunnel

We begin to have periods of hope in the next stage of grief. We begin to feel that we are getting some energy back, we begin sleeping better and eating better. We are no longer as fearful as we once were. Things begin to make sense and we feel that we can begin to be responsible for our own future. In this stage it is important that we have people around us to support us. Others can help us in making the changes necessary to complete the grief process. Healthy people ask for help from others. They can accept love and guidance and this keeps the energy and hope alive in themselves.

In families and people of dependency asking for help is not an option. We have a belief system that says, "I don't need anyone's help, no one is going to tell me what to do because I know what is best for me." Asking for help in these dysfunctional family systems is seen as a weakness or a betrayal. Consequently, this stage of grief becomes short-lived. We go back into one of the previous stages of grief and can stay there for years. This hope stage comes to us only intermittently in our lives. If we do not have support and guidance to help us learn how to change ourselves, the hope dissipates. We begin to doubt that life has happiness in it. Instead, we look at life as a struggle, filled with pain and fear and anger. We feel sorry for those that show some sense of hope that life will get better. We shake our heads and say to ourselves, "If they only knew. They will find out that life is hard."

Others begin to feel a sense of hope and get grand ideas how they will control all others in order for their hope to become a reality. When they find that they have little or no control over others, they will return to one of the other stages of grief. Life brings us grief. It is what we do with the grief that makes it good, bad or indifferent. It is also the difference between a balanced or imbalanced lifestyle.

Our Hit And Wish Lists

The Hit List

The "Hit List" that we form in our heads is a result of the pain we feel. It is the list of people, places and things that we resent, will not accept or will not forgive. Our belief is that the people, places or things on our hit list are in some way responsible for our feelings of pain, anger, fear, loneliness, guilt, etc., the negative feelings. We keep the hit list for a reference in case we need to use, manipulate or blame someone or something for our thoughts, feelings, behaviors or attitudes. We have been taught how to do this by others with dependency. When your father was angry and drinking you listened for hours at him rant and rave about everyone, everything and every place that made him miserable. You listened as your mother lay crying on the sofa blaming people, places and things for her misery. Today you can listen to yourself and become aware that you have many people, places and things on your hit list that match your parents'. On your father's hit list would be his boss, his co-workers, the United States of America, the police department, the President of the United States, his father, his in-laws, money, the state of Florida, etc., etc. On your mother's hit list might be her husband, her father, her mother, her in-laws, you, men, the work force, etc. An example of a typical hit list appears below.

> I blame my mother for not being there for me.
> I blame my mother for using pills.
> I blame my mother for lying to me.
> I blame my mother for not protecting me from my father.
> I blame my father for calling me names.
> I blame my father for not keeping a steady job.
> I blame my father for drinking.
> I blame my father for physically abusing mother.
> I blame my parents for not attending any of my functions in school, etc.
> I blame my friend for not being there for me.
> I blame my co-workers for not being grateful enough for what I do.
> I blame my husband for not communicating with me.
> I blame my husband for not coming home on time.
> I blame my daughter for not appreciating what I do.
> I blame my son for causing trouble in the family.
> I blame the state of Minnesota for making my father drink.
> I blame my place of employment for not giving me a raise.
> I blame the landlord for not understanding about late rent money and embarrassing our family.

> I blame teachers for picking on my children.
> I blame society for being unfair to my husband (making him go to workhouse).
> I blame the car for breaking down on me and I have no money to fix it.
> I blame the banks for not giving me a loan.

The list will be a long one. As you discipline yourself to write down all the items on your hit list you will become aware of the multitude of people, places and things you have been believing have caused you pain, anger, guilt, etc.

There is a second half to this hit list, the excuse part, and this is very important for you to study and record. It works as follows: my mother was not there for me *so I get to*. Now go back over the hit list you have made and add this. Call it "So I get to" because these words will be your excuse system. For example:

> My mother was not there for me so I get to be angry at my husband.
> My father was an alcoholic so I get to be sarcastic and rude to whomever I choose.
> My father physically abused my mother so I get to be crabby and pout, call my husband names, accuse him of being unfaithful, threaten him with divorce whenever I choose, not tell him where I was or am going, give him the silent treatment, withdraw and not tell him what is wrong with me, make him guess and if he is wrong tell him he really does not love me.
> My mother lied to me so I get to lie whenever I want.
> My father called me names so I get to call others names that hurt and they should understand.
> My parents did not attend any of my school functions so I get to be at my children's school more than they do and attempt to make them the most popular children in the school. I get my children involved in as many activities as I choose and if they do not want to I put guilt on them by reminding them their grandparents never came for me.

My friend was not there for me so I get to hurt them by gossiping about them to another person, most likely adding, subtracting or multiplying the truth to make a strong point. When confronted by my friend, I lie and state, "I would never talk about you behind your back."

My daughter doesn't appreciate me so I get to "forget" to wash the blouse she needed.

My husband did not come home in my "time frame" so I get to go out and not tell him where I am going and what time I will be home.

My son caused trouble in the family so I get to yell at him and remind him that he is at fault for making the family look bad. I can do this for years.

Teachers picked on my children so I get to share with my children how unfair society is and how to get back at the teacher and any teacher in the future who might pick on them.

And so the hit list goes on and on. This is an important part of the study of self. If you begin to feel embarrassed by this information about yourself, just know that it is an important part of you and will help in knowing what to change in your attitudes, feelings and behaviors.

I used to pray to God every night to please make my dad stop drinking. I didn't realize that it was my dad's responsibility. I had listened to him and others blame his drinking on everything but himself for years. I became angry because God didn't do what I asked Him to so I put God on my hit list. Then I reasoned that God hadn't made dad stop drinking because I was a bad girl. Guilt set in and I tried to prove I was a good girl so that my father would stop drinking. My father died of alcoholism at the age of 51. It was a horrible death. I was 29 years old and still believed that because I had not been a good enough girl God had taken my dad. I sat with him in the hospital hour after hour, watching him dying in immense pain and sadness. He could not speak the last few days and he would look at me with fear in his eyes. How I wanted to make it all better for him. How sad I was to see my dad, whom I loved dearly, even though he was alcoholic, dying in such a horrible way. After many attempts at begging both my father and God that he not die, he did. I felt I was a failure, became deeply depressed and attempted suicide.

After my dad died, I was so angry and I did not know what to do with this anger, so I put all the blame on God and my mother and I put them at the top of my hit list. I blamed them for everything. Everything that had happened to me in my life that was negative, painful, fearful, angry, etc. I blamed both God and my mother for. I took my dad off my hit list, I told myself that I could no longer be angry with my dad because he was dead. The reality was I was angry at him for many things but, at the time, it was for leaving me. When I wanted to die a few weeks after my dad died, I felt so sorry for myself. I was afraid, I was confused and all I knew for sure was I wanted to be with my dad. What happened was I had put myself on my own hit list and blamed myself for all my dad's pain. I added all my dad's pain to my pain and I deluded myself into thinking everything would be okay if I could die too. My dad wanted to die; he had told me over and over again that he did not want to live any longer. I was different, something in me wanted to live, as I have already shared in this book. I am so glad I had the courage and willingness in me to ask for help, take responsibility for my feelings, behaviors and attitudes, accept guidance and make changes where they were necessary. Due to this, my life now is good. I have done things in my recovery that I would never have believed possible: I have found balance in my life, I can love freely, be loved and live life. So can you; you have the *Magic Within*. If I can do it, so can you.

The Wish List

Many of us survive by retreating into daydreams and fantasies. Many of these often begin with the words, "If only . . .:" If only mom would stop drinking, if only someone would come along and take me away from all this or if only I were good enough, maybe . . . We imagine that if we could only make certain people happy enough, they would stop causing us pain. This is so sad because we believe it's our job to create happiness for others so that they can make us happy. We don't have to make anyone happy except ourselves. We have happiness inside of us, just waiting to be tapped. To find it we have to be responsible enough to let someone take us within and discover where it is. This is the *Magic Within*.

As a child, did you feel free to have friends over for dinner or for a slumber party? Or did you make excuses over your shoulder as you ran home so that no one could put you on the spot? Did you desperately hope that someone would invite you to stay at their house because you knew it would provide a break from the craziness of your house? If you did have friends over, how big of a production did you make it? Were you so tense the whole time that you couldn't enjoy it because of the unpredictability of your dependent family? These are issues many dependents faced as they were growing up and they still affect them in adulthood. They still feel tension at an evening get-together with the neighbors, they make excuses to not attend social events or feel guilty about having a good time. At the same time they fantasize how it could be, should be or would be . . . "If only . . ."

As negative as the hit list is the wish list goes to the other extreme. The wish list also stems from pain and has the ability to stop the pain temporarily. Many of us began this list as children and continue it even as adults, making the statement, "I will never be like my parents, I will never treat my children as they treated me."

> I wish my mother would stop drinking so I could talk to her and she could love me.
> I wish my father would stop yelling so I could go to sleep.
> I wish my family would have fun together so I could tell my friends.
> I wish someone would take me away from this so I could feel loved and not so lonely and scared.

I wish God would answer my prayers and make my father
stop drinking so I wouldn't have to afraid all the time.
I wish my mother would die (anger) so she would stop
embarrassing me.
I wish I had a lot of money so I could do whatever I want
and not need anyone.
I wish I had my own children so I could love them the
way I wanted to loved.
I wish people would stop picking on me so I could stop
being angry.
I wish all alcohol/drugs would be taken off the face of
the earth so people I love would not be so terrible.
I wish people would leave me alone so I could be all by
myself and not talk to anyone, then I wouldn't hurt
so much.

This list, like the hit list, can go on and on and is just as
important to record. You will begin to see a pattern
forming of your belief system stemming from the two
extremes. What you will be working toward is the balance of these extremes but first you have to record the
extremes. Some of them may even seem funny to you. I
might add here that it will be important in your recovery
to learn to laugh and not take everything as seriously as
we tend to. *Lighten up* can be a motto you can remind
yourself of when you get angry and negative with your
recovery process.

When we find ourselves concentrating on either the
wish list or the hit list, we may find that for some reason
we want to take the focus away from ourselves and not
be responsible for what we need to do. Most of the work
we need to do to find balance in our lives is our responsibility. You may find that there are times that you want
someone or something else to do your recovery work for
you. If that happens, you may become aware that you are
using your wish list and you may hear yourself wishing
that "God would . . ." or "mom would . . ." or "someone
would . . ." In reality our wish list is a list of people we
wish would recover for us. When we look at it we will see
what we don't want to be responsible for. If we are not

responsible for the changes in our recovery process then
we would not be able to take the credit and feel the
wonder, peace and freedom of finding the balance.

6

Where Do We Go From Here?

Stages Of Recovery

Recovery is the discovery of self and being responsible for what you find by asking for help, accepting guidance and taking the responsibility to make the changes that are necessary to find the balance in our lives. Recovery is a process which includes healing and change together with finding and maintaining the balance in our lives.

In the process of recovery there are stages we may experience. Each stage is necessary to healing and finding the balance. Each person will experience these stages individually. Some of us will move through each stage integrating them as we are guided. Some of us may experience one stage of recovery and be unable to move on to the next stage or integrate it to find balance due to unwillingness to be responsible for making changes in our lives. Some of us may become fearful of the changes we need to make and not continue on with our recovery.

In each stage of recovery there may be pitfalls or obstacles to overcome. If you are aware of these stages and the possible pitfalls that we, as dependents, may experience, it may be easier for you to recognize where you are in finding the balance and not to be too hard on yourself.

Let's Start At The Very Beginning

There is a period at the beginning of recovery that I call the "excitement period." We have taken the *big* risk and admitted that we need help, we seek out information and find that there are others who think, feel and behave just as we do. We find that we are not alone and we speak to people who have actually changed and their lives are different. There is hope for us. We are so grateful and excited about being able to change and feel better that we want to share this with everyone, whether or not they want to hear it. We gain knowledge and experiences at groups, meetings and educational lectures and we want to tell our families all about what happened. We get so excited about going to these meetings and groups that we tell anyone who will listen about how we are going to find balance in our lives. Then we get carried away and we begin to tell our family members, friends and co-workers how they *must* change so they can feel better. We are so full of hope and excited we want everyone to get into recovery.

In my own recovery I came home from my initial treatment in this excitement and shared my experience with my family. I spoke in treatment language: I hear you saying, you appear to be, etc. I loved everyone and hugged them. I made promises about how different everything would be and how happy we were all going to be. This went on for days. One evening at the dinner table my son, who was then five years old, looked up from his dinner after hearing me go on and on and said, "Mommy, can't you talk right anymore?" I felt hurt and confused. I thought they would all be as excited as I was. What I learned from this experience and with the help of my group is that my recovery is mine and that not everyone is going to be excited about my recovery.

This does not mean you cannot share your joy and excitement with others. It simply means do not push your recovery onto others. They may not be ready for the information, they may still be in denial or delusion. Your recovery may present a threat to them. When we choose to take responsibility for ourselves and want to change, this can cause others to become defensive and they may want you to stay the same so they do not have to become responsible for their own behaviors, feelings and attitudes. They may attempt to get you back into their control by manipulating, blaming, making fun of your recovery, becoming angry and wanting to hurt you.

As you begin to change it will affect others around you whether they choose to change or not. They can feel as if they are losing control and become fearful. Your being responsible for youself and not blaming others and focusing outside of yourself may begin to penetrate their denial and delusion and, if they do not want to change, they will have to defend, deny and delude themselves to stay in the dependency. You may become the family's scapegoat. They may make fun of your recovery and those weird groups and meetings you attend. They may not want to be around you. They will watch you constantly to see if what you are saying matches with your behavior. If you continue on with your recovery, some may want what you have and may begin to ask questions about what you are doing. They may eventually ask what they can do about themselves or if they can go to a meeting with you. Your recovery affects others. It penetrates the denial and delusion of the family system, it brings reality to them about their dependency. Some will choose not to be a part of recovery and will die being dependent and some will make the choice to seek help for themselves.

In my own family system, after 14 years of recovery, about one-third of my family are in recovery, one-third of them died dependent and one-third are not in recovery. But family gatherings are noticeably different and those not in recovery are becoming the minority.

In our process of recovery we will experience pitfalls or obstacles that at the time will feel like failure but you don't have to feel you have failed if you are open to asking for help and learning from your mistakes. These pitfalls or obstacles to recovery strengthen us and give us courage to go on. Healthy people understand that life has positive and negative happenings throughout. They relax and enjoy the positive and gain energy from them so when the negatives happen, and they will, they have the courage and strength to grow and learn from them. It is only the delusion of the dependent that first of all they believe life is pain, fear and suffering and then, when they choose to begin recovery, they believe that life will be all positive and if anything negative happens then we must be failing recovery.

Information Stage

We need to know what is wrong before we can do anything about how to change what is not working for us. This is the information stage. In this stage we seek out and receive information on our dependency. We read books, attend lectures, movies, support groups, listen to tapes and others who are experienced in dependency. We gather all the information we can to begin to identify with our own dependency.

Some people in this stage gather information for others, not themselves. Their belief is that if they can become educated about the dependency, then they can use it to change others. They can recognize all the problems in everyone else and do not recognize their own problems. They may take this information home and use it to confront others to attempt to make them change. They read books to understand others, they listen to tapes to understand others but do very little, if any, analysis of themselves. Their belief is still if I can get others to change, then I will be okay.

Some may use intellectualizing as a defense to protect themselves and get stuck in this stage believing that this is total recovery. They become the know-it-alls of recovery. They may sound great as they quote different books and lecturers and always have the answer for how others need to recover. If they are in group therapy, they can become the group experts or act as if they are the co-therapist. Any chance they get they tell others how much they know about dependency. They can become boring and obnoxious to the people who are moving along in their recoveries. They may seek out the newcomers and beginners in groups and meetings to continue to sound good.

Others gain all the information they can to analyze themselves to find somewhere to place the blame. These people may not go into groups as they feel more comfortable in one-to-one counseling. They do very little about their responsibility to change. They become confused with specifics and may tend to generalize to continue with their analyzing. If they become group members, they give analytical feedback and speak in generalized terms such as we, us, they and them. They rarely use "I" statements. They can sound and appear arrogant, can be hard to get to know and rarely share feelings.

Others seek out all the information they can so that they can begin to identify what it is about them that needs change. They speak from the "I" and begin to take responsibility for their part in the dependency. When they do not understand or become confused, they ask for help and guidance in what they need to change about themselves. These people are sick of being sick and are becoming willing to do whatever is necessary to find the balance in their lives. In groups and meetings they are specific about what they are doing and have the ability to share their experience to help others; they do not attempt to change others. They stay in reality, they confront others with genuine concern, not to be arrogant or a know-it-all. They accept *what is* and apply it to themselves and make the changes necessary to continue with their recovery.

Those people that do not gain the information on dependency to apply it to themselves, ask for help and make the changes, stay in this stage believing that this is total recovery and that they have found the balance to their lives. Not moving through this stage keeps people in an "I know" place. It is safe and there are few risks to be taken. This can be a hard stage to break through because we sound good to ourselves and to others and in the past it has always been important to be right. The cycle can be broken by getting responsible for your own part in dependency, asking for help and making the changes necessary for your recovery. If you stay in the information stage there will no change and balance will not be found. This stage begins your healing but it is not your total healing. Not making changes can be a pitfall or obstacle in recovery. To know what needs to be changed and actually making those changes are two different parts of recovery. We may have the knowledge of what needs change but we do not make a change in our behavior. This can lead us to frustration, which leads us to feeling unworthy, which leads us to self-pity, one of our old friends, and back we can go to feeling that life is pain. Then our old behaviors, feelings and attitudes are just waiting to be put back into our lives. This is the easy way to go; back to what we know best. We need support to continue on.

An *A* in therapy is an *F* in healing and finding the balance. This pitfall finds some people in the belief that if they sound and look good in treatment, group or individual session, they will heal. These people rarely become responsible enough to make change in themselves. They put their whole self into therapy but nothing into changing and finding the balance in their lives. If you happen to be in therapy or a support system meeting with these people, you can easily become bored with what they are saying because there is no evidence of change, only a person who knows how to sound good.

They tend to become know-it-alls and tell everyone else what is best for them.

Feelings Stage

Another stage we will experience in recovery is that of feelings. First of all, we will have to identify and know what our feelings are, then how we have denied and defended these feelings and finally how we learned to avoid as much emotional pain as possible. Specifically, we need to identify how we behaved and what we told ourselves about each feeling.

What did we do when we were angry? How did we sound? What did we say? What did we think?

What did we do when we were sad? How did we sound? What did we say? What did we think?

Many of us have denied our true or gut-level feelings and used our intellect to project the feelings we think we should have. When we begin to study our feelings many may be feelings we think we should have rather than true gut-level feelings. We will need guidance to learn to get to the true feelings. We must go inside our box or trap, identify the feelings, be responsible for having them, discharge them with guidance and get rid of them, clean them out of ourselves. When this process of cleansing begins to happen, it feels good. We can feel lighter, have more energy or not be as tired. Feelings are energy and energy never dies, it just moves from place to place. When people begin to discharge their feelings they may experience some physical symptoms as well.

When I discharged anger with my mother in the movie *Another Chance*, with Sharon Wegscheider-Cruse, it came out as yelling, crying, sobbing and screaming. A few hours after this happened my body felt as if I had been hit by a truck. I was sore all over, even my neck muscles were sore. The energy that was in my body from holding on to the anger had been discharged and I could feel it physically. I was tired but it was not heavy. I felt lighter and somehow excited. There is a sense of great relief. This is good but there are still problems. Some people can become stuck in this discharge phase and want to discharge feelings constantly in this manner to experience relief. We have waited so long to express our feelings that we can become dependent on the relief of it. This is part of healing, as it is time to empty ourselves of these supressed feelings but to be stuck here can be risky. We may overdose ourselves emotionally and this then becomes a pitfall or obstacle to our recovery and finding the balance we need to in order to take responsibility for our feelings as they occur.

The pitfall of this stage is that we believe that we must be suffering all the time. We tell others how we are suffering, we downplay our changes and our good feelings, we have the belief that we do not deserve to feel good until everyone else is happy. We do not deserve this much happiness. This can trap us into an old belief of ours that there is something admirable and noble about suffering, struggling and feeling bad. We can begin to dig for feelings to discharge and many times can even lie about how intense these feelings are. We believe that the louder and more dramatic we are when we discharge our feelings the more we have suffered. We are trapped in this pit because we have not learned how to balance our feelings and still believe that all our feelings must be dramatic and cause us a lot of suffering. Others may become bored with us and confront us about not finding the balance to our feelings. We come to our group over and over again with the same feelings at the same intensity, not letting go of them so that we can feel the relief. Our group can always count on us to do some feeling work if nothing else is happening.

As in all the other areas of our recovery, we should find how to balance our feelings, be responsible for having them, share them and then let go of them and move on to other, more healthy, feelings.

Love Stage

Because there is a sense of relief as a result of the work we've done and because we are beginning to understand and accept ourselves, we start to identify with the pain of others. We begin to understand the pain of the people we once said we hated. This is love, the acceptance and understanding of self and others. This stage develops acceptance, forgiveness and understanding which, in turn, can create feelings of love and being loved. A sense of gratitude will usually develop while working in this stage of recovery. This is gratitude that people can still love us unconditionally, regardless of how we have acted in the past.

Love is a nice word that sends messages to many people in many different ways. There is unconditional love, conditional love, a mother's love, a father's love, tough love, a child's love. The healthy parent feels this unconditional love toward the infant. Then something happens and conditions are put on love. In the dependent or dysfunctional family the message of conditional love comes in many forms: If you loved me you wouldn't, if you loved me you would, how can you do this to me, don't you love me, you don't love me. They are used to manipulate the person they are directed at or make them feel guilty. Messages of conditional love usually make sense to the person directing them because they also have been taught conditional love. There is a strong need to look at how people define the love they are talking about and what expectations they have tied to it. In facilitating a group I have asked people to list feelings, such as when they experience love, and then asked them to define it or explain what they mean by it. Very often they are not sure what love means and then silence will fill the air.

In some cases it is because people are embarrassed by the question or they don't know for sure what their definition is. Some attach this feeling to what they can get from another person in the way of material things, sex or being taken care of. When the others in their life cannot fill their expectations they will be accused of not loving anymore instead of checking out their original definition of love. There is "I love you but I don't like you right now" which doesn't make any sense to the person stuck in their conditional love. They think that if you love me you have to like me too. My alcoholic father and mother caused a lot of hurt in my life. It wasn't until I could admit that I loved them but didn't like what they did that I felt freed from my guilt. It was a relief to find out that I could love.

It is okay to love those that are no longer living if it helps us with what we want to do. We may have some other feelings attached to this love but that is okay. When my father died of alcoholism I was angry at him. When I accepted that alcoholism was a disease I was able to turn my anger toward alcoholism and love him unconditionally. It has always been gratifying to say to a patient, "It's okay to love your — , they did the best they could with what they had." Love toward someone comes from within and is not tied to what we receive. A lesson I learned was to know I could love someone even if they didn't love me. Being able to give someone permission to love unconditionally, to see their eyes light up, tells me it is old attitudes that prevent this person from loving, that it is important for love to be in their life.

Many times dependency is misinterpreted as love. And many times this happens because of old beliefs about what love is, in particular, believing that love is conditional — "if you love me you will take care of me," "if you love me you will never dislike me," "if you love me you will put up with my behavior no matter what it is," "if you love me you will never ask me to change because you love me the way I am" or "I can't live without you." The "I can't live without you" love is one of the most obvious dependency statements used. To say and feel that you can't live without someone's love is dependency and can cause a lot of fear for the person who feels this way. We need to love ourselves in order to love others. Have you thought about this during your struggles? For some it takes therapy, groups, etc. to discover this truth about love.

Love sees, dependency is blind. As with other feelings it needs a lot of attention in order to produce any change in you. It needs to be tied to attitude and behavior. It deserves as much attention as fear, anger, pain, resentment, jealousy, etc., if not more because love has been and will continue to be involved in all these feelings.

Integration

Having worked through the previous stages they now have to be integrated to achieve balance. This balance is healing. The therapist and the group we choose can help guide us through these stages of recovery and then can help us integrate them.

Finding The Balance

I have used the word balance frequently in this book. It has become more and more apparent to me both in my own recovery and in helping others in their recovery that we, as dependents, spend most of our time in extreme behaviors, thoughts and feelings. Dependency is living at the extremes. A chemically dependent person is either preoccupied with finding a way to obtain or use chemicals, they are actually high or drunk or they are hung over and remorseful about their behavior while they were obtaining and using. Most behaviors, feelings and attitudes in the middle of these extremes are never experienced or used by them. This is also the way other dependencies work. We are rigid and controlling and believe in black or white, never gray, good or bad, right or wrong, this or that. However, if this fails to work for us then we become vague so as not to be responsible for anything specific. To work toward health, which is to achieve more balance in our lives, we must know our extremes. You can gain this knowledge through the study of self and by taking the responsibility to ask for guidance and make the changes. In this book I have discussed many of the extremes of dependency. In order to help you further understand, draw a line and put *Minimize* at one end and *Maximize* at the other.

Minimize ——————————————— Maximize

Using your anger as an example, write all the feelings, attitudes and behaviors you use to minimize your anger and record them under the heading Minimize. For example, I minimize my anger by saying I am not angry. I smile so that no one can tell I am angry. I make fun of others by saying I was only kidding. I accidentally bump into someone or pull their arm a little too hard. I tell myself that nothing makes me angry. I expect that you personally can add more to the list on how you minimize anger.

Next, under the heading of Maximize, record the feelings, attitudes and behaviors you use with your anger. For example, I maximize my anger by yelling at people. I call people names and accuse them of things. I think of ways to hurt others and make plans to hurt them, either emotionally, verbally or physically or all three. I leave people out of a conversation because I know it will hurt their feelings. I ignore people, I tell them I had forgotten we had an appointment or date. I constantly remind people how tough and bad I am and that they should not mess with me or there could be trouble. Now you can continue with your list of how you maximize your anger.

Next, record the extremes with hurt. I minimize my hurt by telling myself that this does not bother me, it does not really matter what I think. I make fun of myself before someone else does. I also minimize my hurt by being extra nice to those I feel have hurt me and I always keep smiling so I will not cry. At the other extreme I maximize my hurt when I cry all the time and when someone asks me what the matter is, I tell them and exaggerate the story. I pout until someone asks me what the matter is. I look sad and tired. I isolate myself from others so no one will hurt me again. I tell myself life has no happiness in it for me. I strike out at others so that they will hurt as much as I do. Now record how you maximize your hurt.

Next examine happiness. Some examples of how I minimize my happiness are to act as if I am not enjoying myself, telling myself that it will not last, putting others down that are happy all the time, keeping myself in control so that when the happiness ends, and it will, I will be okay. To maximize happiness I tell everyone how much fun it will be even if they do not want to hear about it, lie to others about how happy I am, attempt to force others to be happy, always have ideas as to how other people can be happy, fantasize about what and who will make me happy and tell others it is really happening in my life. Recored how you minimize and maximize your happiness.

These examples may give you an idea of how to use your study of self to find your extremes. You can use this exercise with all of your feelings, attitudes and behaviors. Remember, be honest. If you find that you become embarrassed or ashamed by what you are recording, continue anyway. These are some of the the things we must face in order to heal. Once you begin to see the extremes, you may see a pattern form and then you, along with your guides, may better understand what you need to do to find your balance. Examining your extremes and finding your balance can be fun once you become responsible.

Making The Changes

Take A Risk

In my early recovery I read every self-help book available. I would begin reading them with great eagerness because I thought they would give me the solutions to all my questions and problems. At that time there was little or no information on dependency or adult children of alcoholics. As I read I would begin to feel disappointed because I felt I was not getting the answers I needed. I believed the directions would be simple, very black and white and direct and I would follow these directions and then everything would be fixed. First of all, I was always reading to find out what to do with the people in my family that were causing me problems, not for myself. I would recognize their problems and get so excited that this book knew what the problem was, that the people in my life were not acting right and this was the reason I was not happy. But then I would read on to find out how to fix the problem and it would be vague and generalized. I would get angry, put the book down and tell myself that there was no hope for me or my family and that no one really understood. I would again feel hopeless until I found a different book and then the same scenario of being excited until I became disappointed once more would occur. Much later in my recovery I began reading books for myself rather than for my family. The directions became clearer but still did not have solutions that I wanted. I told myself that if they could just tell me exactly what I needed to do I would do it. I was always looking for the easiest way to change at no risk for myself.

You may have read this book or others with the same feelings and thoughts. The problem is that when we read we gain knowledge and this is all we do, gain knowledge. But you and I do not know what to do with the knowledge we have gained so we feel disappointed and hopeless. Some people I have met in my recovery are full of knowledge yet they still feel helpless and hopeless. One reason for this is they have failed to ask for help in using the knowledge they have gained. We want so badly to change by ourselves without taking any risks. Unfortunately, changing and working on your recovery is taking risk after risk, asking for guidance, taking a risk, asking for more guidance and taking more risks. We have led a life of risk-taking when we lived with dependency and/or addiction but when it comes to helping ourselves we say that we do not trust the process, therefore we can take no risks. Recovery has to be risk-free with a guaranteed outcome for our good or we will not be willing to do it. We set up a defense that tells others that they must prove to us that we will want this thing called recovery. And the minute that we hear, see or feel something we do not like, we say, "I will not do this or that." We retreat to the place of safety inside ourselves, the trap or box that we have created to protect ourselves and tell ourselves, "I do not need to make the changes they say I need to make, those people do not know what they are talking about, they do not know how I feel, why are they picking on me, they don't really care." Some people stay in their box or trap.

Some of us who slowly become responsible retreat to that trap or box many times in recovery but do not stay there. What we have trusted in our dependencies is the pain, anger, fear, shame, loneliness, etc. We defend and trust the negatives of dependency. We will trust the words of our father the alcoholic before we trust the words of our counselor, psychiatrist or sponsor. It is a matter of changing what you trust. It takes a lot of trust and courage to ask for help the first time, go to a support group meeting, go to a counselor or into intensive treatment. These are all courageous and trusting behaviors. Once we finally get there, we start defending all the negative things and ourselves from the very people we had decided were going to be able to help us. We go inside ourselves and sit in judgment of the place or people we chose for help.

I have always been amazed at this cycle of reaching out then becoming critical. I have found myself doing this. Most people who go into treatment must face many fears. They ask themselves, what will people say? what will they find out about me? will they lock me up? will they tell me I am crazy? will they laugh at me? will they reject me? The questions go on and on. We face these fears and, with our hearts beating heavily in our chests, we pack our luggage, get on an airplane or into the car and take the long journey to the chosen place of treatment. We get to the place of choice and meet many new people that we know nothing about who give us rules and tell us what is expected of us while we are in this place. They introduce us to more people we know nothing about and these people have more rules for us to follow but we face these fears and anxieties and go on. Soon it is time to meet as a group and we go into a room with people we do not know, sit in a circle and look at all the faces and decide within ourselves who we will like and who we will not have anything to do with. Our denial and delusion tells us to defend ourselves by being judgmental. We have faced all these fears and then we are asked to speak and we say, "I cannot stay here and talk in front of this many people" or whichever of the many excuses we give. It is always amazing to me to see this happen but it does. We are so courageous and trusting until we have to be responsible for ourselves and then we back off and refuse to go any farther. At this time some people leave treatment to return to their box or trap. But many stay and become responsible for their fears. They choose to stay and get the help they so desperately want and need.

Take Time

Making changes takes time. I know some of you do not want to hear this but it is the truth. We go back to our wish list and wish we could get well in 8, 10, 21 or 28 days. That is merely the beginning of the process. Treatment is where we are given the tools of recovery so that we can become responsible for ourselves and put them to use in making the necessary changes in ourselves. After the initial treatment we will need *continual* guidance in many different ways and in many different areas to find the balance we need to find. This does not mean that the more treatments you attend the healthier you are.

Some people become treatment junkies. They go into some form of treatment whether it is a long-term intensive, or a conference or a workshop every time they feel unsure or not safe. Sometimes they become dependent on the feeling of "love" they feel in these places or the sense of security they believe these places provide for them. They can even become dependent on the treatment technique that is used. Over and over again they go off to treatment and fail to see the irresponsibility in this. Some of these people have told me that it became too frightening for them to continue on the outside so they compulsively sought out another treatment. What generally happens with these people is that every time life gives them a big chunk of responsibility to handle they become frightened and seek safety and to these particular people, safety is in a treatment setting. Over a period of time they are unable to make any decisions without treatment and this enables them to continue with their irresponsible behavior.

To make changes in your life you will need to know what you do and how you do it before you will know what needs to be changed. When you find out what needs to be changed, it will be necessary for you to get the guidance on how to change. Then you will need help on being specific and "chunking" it down so that you will know and feel the change. These changes are concrete and simplistic. It is very important that you know the changes really are happening. If a suggested change seems too much for you then be honest and tell your chosen guide. Specific changes are easier to be responsible for and they feel manageable even though they may be scary.

Be Specific

I have given some examples of specific changes earlier in this book and will list more so they are easier for you understand.

Just Say No

Say no to something you always used to say yes to. I always said yes to everything even if I did not want to do it. It was a change for me to say no when I did not want to do something. Saying no was scary because I felt no one would love me if I did not agree to everything. One day I took responsibility for myself and told my cousin that I did not want to babysit for her children. She was shocked because I never said no before and she asked me, "What did you say?" My heart was pounding with fear but I repeated that I would not babysit. Then she said, "Okay, I will call you later." I was as shocked as she was and for days afterwards I felt guilty.

I brought this to my group and they told me I should say no again when I did not want to do something. I did this and I began to feel good about having a choice. Then I did what most of us do and went from one extreme to the other before I could find the balance. I said no to everything because it felt so good. Even if I wanted to say yes, I said no and I did not feel guilty or fearful. I felt good. Soon I began to find the balance and now I know how to be responsible for my choice. Not everyone liked it when I said no because they were so used to me saying yes, so then they would try to manipulate me to do what they wanted. When they found I could not be manipulated they stopped trying. Later some of these people told me they were actually glad that I could now say no.

Hear No Evil, Speak No Evil

Many of us are sarcastic when we are angry or we gossip and want to keep secrets from others so we have a sense of control over ourselves and others. One way to begin change in this area is very simple. Tell others that you will no longer participate in gossip. Someone would ask me, "Did you hear about so and so?" I would then reply, "I do not want to know what it is unless I can tell the person you are talking about. I do not keep secrets anymore." At first they would give me a funny look and would continue, then I would repeat it, both so I could hear myself and to tell the other person. This was very frightening for me because I was afraid that it would mean that I would have no friends. Also it meant that I had to take a risk and believe that I wanted to be healthy. The others involved who were not undergoing recovery could not understand and would smirk or simply ignore me.

We need to continue with the change so that both we and the people around us understand what we are changing. This will take repeated effort on our part until the change becomes part of us, just as denial and delusion had been a part of us in our dependency. Other people, places and things do not have to change for us and we can still be in recovery. It is so easy for us to quit and go back to old behaviors, feelings and attitudes, not because they are good for us, nor because we want to stay sick but because they are more a part of us than the new change. It is like starting a new job. At first everything seems complicated and strange. The language is different, the people we work with are different, the schedule is different but we continue going to work day after day and doing what is different until one day it becomes a part of us. Then we cannot understand why we thought it was so hard at first.

In recovery there will be many times when you feel disappointed or tired or fearful or confused; this is only natural. What needs to be done when this happens is to have support from others who understand what you are feeling and can give you some guidance as to how to continue with your recovery. I have heard so often from people that recovery is just too hard. If confusion sets in and we become fearful and naturally go back to what we know, do not be too hard on yourselves; just know that it is time for more guidance and support. You are not failing recovery, you are moving to a different stage. You are growing and becoming healthier each time this occurs. If a change you have been working on for a time is just not going anywhere, put it aside for a short time while you work on other changes and then, when you become stronger, go back to that change and see what you can do. You will feel the difference. Many times in our arrogance and desire to hurry up and get well as soon as possible we attempt to do more than we can handle, then get disgusted with ourselves and return to old behaviors and attitudes, especially the old attitude that life is a struggle. Each small change that you make builds up your strength to go on to the next change. It is important that you take rest periods in your recovery to gain strength to go on to whatever is next. However, this does not mean resting for years after making a change.

The Great Outdoors

It was important in my recovery to be outside with nature and be a part of it. This was a big change for me. In dependency we feel burdened down and tired much of the time. If you study your habits you will find that being outside is not something you do often. We feel so tired that we spend our time lying on the sofa or in bed watching TV. I honestly would be outside only to go from one destination to the other. In my early recovery I was told to be outside, sitting quietly and watching and listening to nature for three minutes each day at whatever time I choose. I chose the morning and though I thought this guidance was stupid I did what I was told. I took my watch, sat in a chair and looked around, becoming anxious because I thought it was such a long time. I tapped my fingers waiting for the three minutes to be up. I told my counselor that I thought this change was wasting my time (after all, I had so much to do caretaking others). My counselor told me to do it again but this time for five minutes.

Gradually as the weeks went by I began to hear birds singing and I took time to listen to them. I looked at the leaves on the trees becoming aware that they were each a single piece; in my dependency I had just seen a green mass on the trees. I looked at the grass and began to notice butterflies, bees, caterpillars and many other things that I had been oblivious to in my anxiety and dependency. I went to the beach and sat in the sand and let it flow through my fingers. I began picking up shells and noticing how they were shaped. As I took more time to be outside I noticed much of my anxiety about wasting time that I had felt in the beginning was gone, and I even began looking forward to my time outside with nature.

In the various treatment centers that I have been a part of professionally I have always included in the program time to be outside. I would hear the patients grumble about how stupid going outside was to them and I would smile because, sure enough, by the end of their treatment they were beginning to enjoy being outside with nature. As you make this change be sure to record in your journal how you react to being outside with nature because it is fun to go back and see how we have changed. Also, I have read that the sun and light have been found to lift depression and that nature absorbs emotion putting us in a place of peace and tranquility for a time. Try this yourself; be outside and become aware of what surrounds you and see how much fun it is.

Support, Not Advice

Another specific change that I had to work through was to stop telling others how they should live their lives. Many of us find it easy to tell others what to do and at times we give sound advice and have given good direction. This external focus, however, does not do much for our recovery and the anger that we feel when people do not do what we have directed them to do is not healthy for us. In order to change this, listen to others telling you about their problems and say nothing. If they specifically ask for your direction tell them you do not know what they should do. Reassure them that you will support them in whatever they choose to do but refuse to tell them what to do. This will be tough for those of you who obtain your self-worth from telling others what to do but do it anyway. After a time you will notice you will not be as anxious around people or as defensive and you will actually begin to enjoy being with others, when in the past you felt tired and drained. This worked for me and it can for you too.

These are just some examples for you to begin to understand how to make specific changes. Remember to use your guides when you are making these changes in your recovery. There will come a time when you will recognize that a change is needed and you will make the change. However, early in recovery we are so anxious to make everything change that we need constant direction. Have a great time in making your changes and then celebrate your success in changing.

Chunking It Down

It is important in the study of yourself and in your recovery process to keep things in small manageable chunks. If we do not do this, recovery becomes overwhelming and we give up easily, believing we can never feel any different than we always have.

People often make statements such as: I am working on my anger, I am dealing with my issues, I am working on my feelings, I am working though my relationships. These are huge problem areas and can be broken down so as to become more manageable with the added bonus of making the change more noticeable when it occurs. When I say I am dealing with my issues, what does that mean? What specific issue am I dealing with, what is the issue and what does dealing with mean? Many times I have confronted someone about this and they cannot tell me specifically what they are doing. For some this is a way of ducking responsibility. It sounds as if they are working on recovery so people leave them alone but it usually does not mean anything. If we were to follow these people in their recovery we would see that they become frustrated and unable to share how they are changing, if they are changing at all.

To feel the changes we are making is important. It is what gives us self-worth and the courage to go on to the next change. The inner self is saying, "Go for it" and we become excited about what is next. Others notice the change and give us support to move on to make the next change.

An Example

To chunk things down is to keep things specific. When you are working on your pain what particular piece of pain are you working on? The pain you have because your father lied to you, the pain you have when your mother would be drunk, the pain you have about your parents not coming to any of the school functions you were involved in? When you work on a specific piece break it down into smaller pieces. For instance, pain I have because my father lied to me has caused me to feel unloved and angry. When I feel this way I treat others with anger through sarcasm and righteousness. Now you can see what *you* need to work on — your sarcasm and righteousness when you feel unloved. What can you do to change this? Ask for help as to how to stop being sarcastic and righteous from someone who has been through this and can give you specific direction. Ask your counselor, your group members, your sponsor or whatever guide you choose. Record in your journal the guidance you were given, what changes you made and the outcome of these. This is very helpful for future reference to know what worked and what did not.

Now the next area that caused pain. The pain I felt when my mother was drunk has caused me to hate her and be angry. When I feel this way I punish her by yelling at her and calling her names and treat all women who remind me of my mother with anger by being arrogant and condescending. What specific changes are needed to work through this pain?

Next is the pain I felt because my parents did not attend any of the school functions I was in. This has caused me anger and hurt. When I feel this way I do not show up for functions they have planned, i.e. Thanksgiving, birthdays, etc. I want them to hurt just as they hurt me. I say hurtful things to them and remind them of how awful they are as parents. What changes are needed here?

Chunking it down can be used in any of the changes we make in our healing. If it feels too big or you become overwhelmed with the change, ask for more guidance to chunk it down even more. In our eagerness to heal we tend to take on more than we can handle. Remember, we are the type of people that once we ask for help we expect to be healed yesterday.

Now that you have some idea of how to chunk it down, the other changes should come with your being honest about how you feel, think and behave, sharing this with others and asking for help. You will be amazed how easy making changes becomes when you keep them in manageable chunks that you can recognize and take the responsibility to make the changes necessary.

CONCLUSION

You've Got The Magic!

For many of us the experience of feeling good, happy, at peace and balanced will be a new one. I have experienced this and have been told that, as we begin to clear out the negative, we are unsure of what to do with all the new energy we gain. Some people have shared that they feel bored or fearful of the new experience. Our own recovery will bring many new choices and discoveries. We will feel, think and behave very differently. When we become responsible for our own future, whatever life brings us, we will be able to make choices and have many new experiences. It actually can become exciting. No longer do we have to fear the unknown or the beginning of a new day. We can look at them and truly know that we are in charge of our own feelings, attitudes and behaviors. No longer do we have to give ourselves away to dependency. We can learn to accept reality and be responsible for it. We no longer have to depend on outside sources to make us happy. We can learn to accept, forgive and understand ourselves and others. This is true freedom and it belongs to each one of us. It is mine. It is yours. You do deserve happiness. Life, although sometimes unfair, will be what you make it. You cannot change your parents, spouses, children or anyone else but you can change yourself.

I believe that there is positive, healthy energy in all of us. It is energy that gives us courage to ask for help, follow guidance and make changes. This energy has been gnawing at us for a long time, telling us to do something. It is this energy that is the *Magic Within*. In the beginning of our recoveries it is faint and only whispers while the dependency screams and yells. We may need to listen very hard to hear the *Magic Within* but as we heal and clear ourselves out, the *Magic Within* will get louder and stronger.

In my own recovery, I am amazed when I look back in retrospect and see how different I am now; very little is the same. My fear is different, my anger is different, my pain, when it comes up, is different. I have had many painful, fearful experiences in my recovery but I get through them and they clear up. They do not linger and burden me as they did in the past. I look different, I feel different and I behave differently. Many people ask me how long ago the film *Another Change* was made. When I reply that it has been years, they tell me that I look younger now. It's really great to hear that.

I had another wonderful experience just last year when I was given the opportunity to be a co-chair of a big conference with a dear friend. It was held in a beautiful old Victorian hotel. The attendance was way over what was expected. Many of my friends came to be present. There were people there whom I had helped in treatment numbering into the hundreds. As we greeted each other we reminisced, we cried, we laughed and we hugged each other, feeling great love and gratitude. I could hardly believe that all this was happening to me. What wonder, what joy, what a celebration! At the end of the conference I was up on the stage in front of hundreds of people and I had the privilege of introducing all the members of my family. As each of them came on stage I cried with joy. My mother who has been recovering for five years, my brother Tom, recovering for 18 years, my sister Cathy, recovering for four years, my husband Denny, recovering for one year, my daughter Kris, recovering for one year and my son Tom recovering for one year. If someone would have told me ten years ago that this was going to happen, I would not have been able to believe it. Here they all were on stage with me, crying, hugging and loving each other, each one responsible for themself, each one now able to feel, think and behave with freedom and choice.

As we stood up there, each holding hands, I shared with the audience my joy and asked them to have courage to begin their own recovery. That is how it started in my family. My brother Tom was the first to get help and then each of us took the responsibility for our own recoveries. I just knew that as we stood there that my dad and my grandmother were watching filled with happiness and gratitude.

You too can have the experiences of recovery that I have had. Don't give up on yourself or the people you love.

The conference ended with all of us holding hands and singing a song that says, "It's in every one of us to be wise, find your heart, open up both your eyes. We can all know everything, without ever knowing why. It's in every one of us by and by."

Remember, you have the *Magic Within.* Have a wonderful time finding it and enjoying the freedom that comes with it.

Because I Care,
Mary Lee

Books from . . .
Health Communications

AFTER THE TEARS: *Reclaiming The Personal Losses of Childhood*
Jane Middelton-Moz and Lorie Dwinell
Your lost childhood must be grieved in order for you to recapture your
self-worth and enjoyment of life. This book will show you how.
ISBN 0-932194-36-2   **$7.95**

HEALING YOUR SEXUAL SELF
Janet Woititz
How can you break through the aftermath of sexual abuse and enter into
healthy relationships? Survivors are shown how to recognize the problem
and deal effectively with it.
ISBN 1-55874-018-X   **$7.95**

RECOVERY FROM RESCUING
Jacqueline Castine
Effective psychological and spiritual principles teach you when to take
charge, when to let go, and how to break the cycle of guilt and fear that
keeps you in the responsibility trap. Mind-altering ideas and exercises will
guide you to a more carefree life.
ISBN 1-55874-016-3   **$7.95**

ADDICTIVE RELATIONSHIPS: Reclaiming Your Boundaries
Joy Miller
We have given ourselves away to spouse, lover, children, friends or
parents. By examining where we are, where we want to go and how to get
there, we can reclaim our personal boundaries and the true love of
ourselves.
ISBN 1-55874-003-1   **$7.95**

RECOVERY FROM CO-DEPENDENCY:
It's Never Too Late To Reclaim Your Childhood
Laurie Weiss, Jonathan B. Weiss
Having been brought up with life-repressing decisions, the adult child
recognizes something isn't working. This book shows how to change
decisions and live differently and fully.
ISBN 0-932194-85-0   **$9.95**

SHIPPING/HANDLING: All orders shipped UPS unless weight exceeds 200 lbs., special routing is requested, or
delivery territory is outside continental U.S. Orders outside United States shipped either Air Parcel Post or Surface
Parcel Post. Shipping and handling charges apply to all orders shipped whether UPS, Book Rate, Library Rate, Air
or Surface Parcel Post or Common Carrier and will be charged as follows. Orders less than $25.00 in value add
$2.00 minimum. Orders from $25.00 to $50.00 in value (after discount) add $2.50 minimum. Orders greater than
$50.00 in value (after discount) add 6% of value. Orders greater than $25.00 outside United States add 15% of
value. We are not responsible for loss or damage unless material is shipped UPS. Allow 3-5 weeks after receipt of
order for delivery. Prices are subject to change without prior notice.

Enterprise Center, 3201 S.W. 15th Street,
Deerfield Beach, FL 33442-8124
1-800-851-9100

Health
Communications, Inc.

Other Books By . . .
Health Communications

ADULT CHILDREN OF ALCOHOLICS
Janet Woititz
Over a year on *The New York Times* Best-Seller list, this book is the primer on Adult Children of Alcoholics.
ISBN 0-932194-15-X   **$6.95**

STRUGGLE FOR INTIMACY
Janet Woititz
Another best-seller, this book gives insightful advice on learning to love more fully.
ISBN 0-932194-25-7   **$6.95**

DAILY AFFIRMATIONS: For Adult Children of Alcoholics
Rokelle Lerner
These positive affirmations for every day of the year paint a mental picture of your life as you choose it to be.
ISBN 0-932194-27-3   **$6.95**

CHOICEMAKING: For Co-dependents, Adult Children and Spirituality Seekers — Sharon Wegscheider-Cruse
This useful book defines the problems and solves them in a positive way.
ISBN 0-932194-26-5   **$9.95**

LEARNING TO LOVE YOURSELF: Finding Your Self-Worth
Sharon Wegscheider-Cruse
"Self-worth is a choice, not a birthright," says the author as she shows us how we can choose positive self-esteem.
ISBN 0-932194-39-7   **$7.95**

BRADSHAW ON: THE FAMILY: A Revolutionary Way of Self-Discovery
John Bradshaw
The host of the nationally televised series of the same name shows us how families can be healed and individuals can realize full potential.
ISBN 0-932194-54-0   **$9.95**

HEALING THE CHILD WITHIN:
Discovery and Recovery for Adult Children of Dysfunctional Families
Charles Whitfield
Dr. Whitfield defines, describes and discovers how we can reach our Child Within to heal and nurture our woundedness.
ISBN 0-932194-40-0   **$8.95**

Enterprise Center, 3201 S.W. 15th Street,
Deerfield Beach, FL 33442
1-800-851-9100

Health Communications, Inc.

Daily Affirmation Books from . . .
Health Communications

GENTLE REMINDERS FOR CO-DEPENDENTS: Daily Affirmations
Mitzi Chandler
With insight and humor, Mitzi Chandler takes the co-dependent and the adult child through the year. Gentle Reminders is for those in recovery who seek to enjoy the miracle each day brings.
ISBN 1-55874-020-1   **$6.95**

TIME FOR JOY: Daily Affirmations
Ruth Fishel
With quotations, thoughts and healing energizing affirmations these daily messages address the fears and imperfections of being human, guiding us through self-acceptance to a tangible peace and the place within where there is *time for joy.*
ISBN 0-932194-82-6   **$6.95**

CRY HOPE: Positive Affirmations For Healthy Living
Jan Veltman
This book gives positive daily affirmations for seekers and those in recovery. Every day is a new adventure, and change is a challenge.
ISBN 0-932194-74-5   **$6.95**

SAY YES TO LIFE: Daily Affirmations For Recovery
Father Leo Booth
These meditations take you through the year day by day with Father Leo Booth, looking for answers and sometimes discovering that there are none. Father Leo tells us, "For the recovering compulsive person God is too important to miss — may you find Him now."
IBN 0-932194-46-X   **$6.95**

DAILY AFFIRMATIONS: For Adult Children of Alcoholics
Rokelle Lerner
Affirmations are a way to discover personal awareness, growth and spiritual potential, and self-regard. Reading this book gives us an opportunity to nurture ourselves, learn who we are and what we want to become.
ISBN 0-932194-47-3
(Little Red Book)   **$6.95**
(New Cover Edition)   **$6.95**

Enterprise Center, 3201 S.W. 15th Street,
Deerfield Beach, FL 33442
1-800-851-9100

Health Communications, Inc.

New Books . . .
from Health Communications

HEALING THE SHAME THAT BINDS YOU
John Bradshaw
Toxic shame is the core problem in our compulsions, co-dependencies and addictions. The author offers healing techniques to help release the shame that binds us.
ISBN 0-932194-86-9   **$9.95**

THE MIRACLE OF RECOVERY:
Healing For Addicts, Adult Children and Co-dependents
Sharon Wegscheider-Cruse
Beginning with recognizing oneself as a survivor, it is possible to move through risk and change to personal transformation.
ISBN 1-55874-024-4   **$9.95**

CHILDREN OF TRAUMA: Rediscovering Your Discarded Self
Jane Middelton-Moz
This beautiful book shows how to discover the source of past traumas and grieve them to grow into whole and complete adults.
ISBN 1-55874-014-7   **$9.95**

New Books on Spiritual Recovery . . .

LEARNING TO LIVE IN THE NOW: 6-Week Personal Plan To Recovery
Ruth Fishel
The author gently introduces you step by step to the valuable healing tools of meditation, positive creative visualization and affirmations.
ISBN 0-932194-62-1   **$7.95**

CYCLES OF POWER: A User's Guide To The Seven Seasons of Life
Pamela Levin
This innovative book unveils the process of life as a cyclic pattern, providing strategies to use the seven seasons to regain power over your life.
ISBN 0-932194-75-3   **$9.95**

MESSAGES FROM ANNA: Lessons in Living (Santa Claus, God and Love)
Zoe Rankin
This is a quest for the meaning of "love." In a small Texas Gulf Coast town a wise 90-year-old woman named Anna shares her life messages.
ISBN 1-55874-013-9   **$7.95**

THE FLYING BOY: Healing The Wounded Man
John Lee
A man's journey to find his "true masculinity" and his way out of co-dependent and addictive relationships, this book is about feelings — losing them, finding them, expressing them.
ISBN 1-55874-006-6   **$7.95**

Enterprise Center, 3201 S.W. 15th Street,
Deerfield Beach, FL 33442
1-800-851-9100

 **Health Communications, Inc.**